Measuring the Costs
of Visible Protection
in Korea

NAMDOO KIM

Measuring the Costs of Visible Protection in Korea

Institute for International Economics
Washington, DC
Korea Institute for International Economic Policy
Seoul, Korea
November 1996

Namdoo Kim is currently Professor of International Economics at Inje University in Kimhae, South Korea. He was a Research Fellow and Director of Research Coordination at the Korean Institute for International Economic Policy (KIEP) in Seoul between 1989 and 1995. He has been a member of the Korean Tariff Deliberation Commission since 1988. Kim has authored and co-authored a number of books and articles including *Trade Barriers in the United States* (1992), *Direct Investment Flows between the United States and Korea* (1991), and *Long-Term Trends in U.S. Trade Policies* (1990), all published by KIEP in Korean.

INSTITUTE FOR INTERNATIONAL ECONOMICS
11 Dupont Circle, NW
Washington, DC 20036-1207
(202) 328-9000 FAX: (202) 328-0900
http://www.iie.com

C. Fred Bergsten, *Director*
Christine F. Lowry, *Director of Publications*

Typesetting and printing by Automated Graphic Systems

For reprints/permission to photocopy please contact the APS customer service department at CCC Academic Permissions Service, 27 Congress Street, Salem, MA 01970.

Printed in the United States of America
98 97 96   5 4 3 2 1

Library of Congress Cataloging-in-Publication Data

Kim, Namdoo.
Measuring the costs of visible protection in Korea / Namdoo Kim.
   p. cm
Includes bibliographical references (p.   ).
   1. Protectionism—Korea (South)
2. Tariff—Korea (South) 3. Korea (South)—Commercial policy.
4. Commercial products—Korea (South) I. Institute for International Economics (U.S.) II. Taeoe Kyŏngje Chŏngch' aek Yŏn 'guwŏn (Korea) III. Title.
HF2370.5.Z7K56   1996
382'.73'095195—dc20   96-35401
                                        CIP

ISBN 0-88132-236-9

The views expressed in this publication are those of the author. This publication is part of the overall program of the Institute, as endorsed by its Board of Directors, but does not necessarily reflect the views of individual members of the Board or the Advisory Committee.

Contents

Preface   **vii**

1 Introduction and Executive Summary   **1**
Why Study the Costs of Protection?   1
The Challenging Case of Korea   2
Key Findings Regarding Visible Protection Costs   5
Sectoral Comparison and Evaluation   7
Organization of the Remainder of the Study   8

2 Trade Protection in Korea   **9**
Recent Trends in Trade Liberalization   9
Trade Protection by Sector   15
Highly Protected Sectors in 1992   29

3 Estimation Results, Limitations, and Future Research   **33**
Results of Estimation   33
Comparison with Previous Studies   51
Limitations of This Report and Future Research Directions   55
Conclusions   56

Appendix A Measuring the Costs of Korea's Visible Trade Protection in 1992: The Methodology   **57**

Appendix B   **85**

References   **95**

Preface

This study continues the Institute's evaluation of import protection in major economies around the world. The series started with examinations of the United States and Japan (Gary Clyde Hufbauer and Kimberly Ann Elliott, *Measuring the Costs of Protection in the United States*, 1994; and Yoko Sazanami, Shujiro Urata, and Hiroki Kawai, *Measuring the Costs of Protection in Japan*, 1995). This volume by Professor Namdoo Kim analyzes Korea's visible trade barriers and their effects on consumers and producers in Korea. Future studies, now being carried out by colleagues in the respective countries, will examine trade protection in Australia, Canada, China, the European Union, and Indonesia. The overall project is being coordinated by Gary Clyde Hufbauer, Reginald Jones Senior Fellow at the Institute.

These studies are intended to help policymakers assess the impact of tariffs, quotas, and other trade restraints by quantifying their economic costs. Professor Kim uses a methodology similar to that deployed in our previously published study of US protection. Due to data and methodological limitations, however, the study addresses only the *visible* barriers to trade in Korea—tariffs in all sectors and agricultural quotas. It does not cover nontariff measures, which are often alleged to limit imports of manufactured products and services into Korea.

This study is also a part of the Institute's broader project on the Asia Pacific region, a central goal of which is to assess the potential benefits of liberalization in the APEC countries and to make appropriate policy recommendations. Within that framework, the Korea Institute for International Economic Policy (KIEP) and the Institute for International Economics launched several joint analyses in July 1994. The first result of KIEP-IIE cooperation is the present volume on the cost of visible protection in Korea. A study on the financial services sector has also been undertaken by participants from KIEP and the Institute. We are delighted that this joint research has expanded the opportunities to exchange views on APEC between US and Korean economists as well as to deepen the cooperative relationship between KIEP and the Institute for International Economics.

The Institute for International Economics is a private nonprofit institution for the study and discussion of international economic policy. Its purpose is to analyze important issues in that area and to develop and communicate practical new approaches for dealing with them. The Institute is completely nonpartisan.

The Institute is funded largely by philanthropic foundations. Major institutional grants are now being received from the German Marshall Fund of the United States, which created the Institute with a generous commitment of funds in 1981, and from the Ford Foundation, the Andrew Mellon Foundation, and the C. V. Starr Foundation. A number of other foundations and private corporations also contribute to the highly diversified financial resources of the Institute. About 16 percent of the Institute's resources in our latest fiscal year were provided by contributors outside the United States, including about 6 percent from Japan. The Institute's overall project on Asia Pacific economic cooperation is receiving generous support from the Rockefeller Brothers Fund; the AT&T, GE, Pew, and Sasakawa Peace Foundations; and the IBM Corporation. This study was partially financed by the Korea Foundation and the Korea Institute for Economic Policy itself.

The Board of Directors bears overall responsibility for the Institute and gives general guidance and approval to its research program—including identification of topics that are likely to become important to international economic policymakers over the medium run (generally, one to three years), and which thus should be addressed by the Institute. The Director, working closely with the staff and outside Advisory Committee, is responsible for the development of particular projects and makes the final decision to publish an individual study.

The Institute hopes that its studies and other activities will contribute to building a stronger foundation for international economic policy around the world. We invite readers of these publications to let us know how they think we can best accomplish this objective.

C. FRED BERGSTEN
Director
October 1996

Acknowledgments

This study began in the autumn of 1994 as part of a joint research project between the Institute for International Economics and the Korea Institute for International Economic Policy (KIEP) when I was a research fellow at KIEP. I would like to thank Jang-Hee Yoo, the president of KIEP, who initiated the plan for this study and encouraged me to complete it after I left KIEP to take a professorship at Inje University.

During the course of this study, I benefited greatly from many people at the two institutes. First, I would express my deepest appreciation to Gary Hufbauer, who gave me general advice and insightful comments. I would also like to thank other staff members at the Institute for International Economics, including Kimberly Elliott, Gautam Jaggi, Gena Morgan, and Daniel Rosen, who carefully read the manuscript and commented extensively on it.

Korean scholars and government officials made valuable comments on an early draft at a KIEP seminar in May 1995. Research assistants at KIEP were indispensable to this study. Kyu-Young Chai worked hard to collect data and carry out the complex computations. I am very grateful to Sang-Sim Kim and Mi-Sun Lee, who showed a great deal of patience in typing several drafts of the manuscript.

Thank you all for your concerted efforts.

Namdoo Kim

Introduction and Executive Summary

Why Study the Costs of Protection?

Many countries regulate external trade for various economic policy objectives, such as sustaining domestic employment, improving the trade balance, and nurturing infant industries. Protective measures can take the form of import tariffs and quotas, manipulation of exchange rates, buy-national regulations on government procurement, and still other, less transparent restrictions.

Trade protection can prompt foreign countries to slow their own trade liberalization plans, to expend time and effort haggling for redress, or in extreme cases to retaliate for perceived mistreatment. Whatever the foreign response, protection usually hinders the efficient allocation of resources in the protected country itself, thereby reducing national income.[1] Traditional economic theory accordingly recommends a policy of trade liberalization, which enables a more efficient allocation of resources in all countries.

To promote freer trade on a multilateral basis, nearly five decades of continuous effort have been centered on the General Agreement on Tariffs and Trade (GATT). The effort has paid off, and trade barriers have been steadily reduced. As a consequence of the Uruguay Round of multilateral trade negotiations, the new World Trade Organization (WTO) was launched, encompassing the familiar GATT, a new General Agreement

---

1. Successful infant industry protection must be noted as an exception to this rule in a dynamic sense.

on Trade in Services (GATS), and an Agreement on Trade-Related Aspects of Intellectual Property Rights (the TRIPs agreement). Thought is already being given to a new WTO round that would further liberalize trade and investment on a multilateral basis.

Regional liberalization plans have also flourished. In the Asia Pacific region, for example, an ambitious plan of liberalization was embraced in 1994 by the Asia Pacific Economic Cooperation forum (APEC), with target dates of complete liberalization by developed-country members in the year 2010, and developing-country members in 2020.

These trends suggest that most countries will implement full-scale trade and investment liberalization policies within the next two decades. To understand the consequences, it is important for each nation to estimate quantitatively the effects of its existing trade measures and thus the potential benefits of liberalizing its own protective apparatus.

The Challenging Case of Korea

This report evaluates the extent of trade protection in Korea and then quantitatively evaluates the costs of major trade measures.[2] My intention is to provide the general public with a better understanding of the effects of trade protection, thereby enlisting public support for trade liberalization in Korea.

The scope of the research is limited in several important ways (for details, please refer to the description of the model and data in appendix A).

First, this study does not cover all protective measures but instead focuses on "visible" protection of important product sectors. By "visible" protection, I mean tariffs and publicly declared quotas that can be evaluated in tariff-equivalent terms. The antithesis of visible protection is "hidden" protection, especially nontariff barriers (NTBs) on industrial products. In studies of other countries, opaque NTBs have been shown to be both important and difficult to quantify. Because of data and time constraints, Korean NTBs (other than agricultural quotas) are not addressed in this study. Box 1.1 and table 1.1 offer a thumbnail sketch of these less visible types of protection and their relevance for Korea.

Second, this study does not attempt to calculate the effects of protection in Korea for service sectors, though they play a key role in the Korean economy. Service sectors, such as telecommunications, insurance, banking, and civil aviation—to name the most important—are increasingly the subject of international trade negotiations. Again, time and data constraints prevented attention to them in this study. However, Hoekman

---

2. For a description of the measurement of average tariff levels used in this study, see box A.1 in the appendix (p. 64).

Box 1.1 Invisible nontariff barriers in Korea

In measuring the costs of protection in any economy, the "visible" forms of protection are only part of the story. Hidden costs in the form of nontariff barriers (NTBs), which serve to limit import quantities, can play a large or even dominant role in determining total welfare and efficiency losses. Many foreign observers think that this is true for Korea.

NTBs take many forms, including:

- measures to control the volume of imports;
- measures to control the price of imports;
- monitoring measures;
- technical barriers to trade.

Analysis by the APEC Secretariat based on UNCTAD data concluded that the Korean economy in 1993 was marked by global quotas, use of antidumping laws as an NTB, duties, and price undertakings. In the report's frequency analysis, however, Korea showed a fairly low level of tradeables subject to significant NTBs (1.7 percent). Other sources have been more bold in their allegations (table 1.1).

The most difficult challenge is dealing with barriers that are not visible. Such NTBs can be assessed from several directions. First, anecdotal evidence can be amassed in areas such as unfair business practices. For example, the *US Foreign Trade Barriers Report* cites allegations made by US firms in Korea concerning inappropriate pressure upon them to cooperate in distorting markets. Other analysts (e.g., Noland 1996) support such allegations as well.

A second approach, applied by Hoekman (1995), is to draw conclusions from the service activities that national trade negotiators were not willing to bind in the GATS negotiations. This approach requires assumptions about the maximum level of service sector protection and other variables.

A third approach involves a comparison between domestic and world prices. This approach was used in a previous study in this series, dealing with Japanese protection (Sazanami, Urata, and Kawai 1995). Japanese sectors with high implied nontariff barrier rates of protection included, for example, food and beverages (272 percent), metal products (59 percent), chemical products (127 percent), and machinery (140 percent). These sectors may be subject to similar opaque NTBs in Korea. Such data are very difficult to obtain, particularly in manufacturing sectors where quality and transaction conditions vary significantly across countries. Largely for this reason, such an approach was used only for a limited number of agricultural products in this study.

Sources: APEC Secretariat 1995; Sazanami, Urata, and Kawai 1995.

(1995) has estimated very high tariff-equivalent levels of service-sector protection by Korea, just as in other countries (table 1.1). Future studies may show that the less visible types of protection, both for industrial products and services, play a *dominant* role in determining the total costs of protection in Korea.

Table. 1.1   Allegations on implicit nontariff barriers in Korea[a]

Source	Basis	Allegation
USTR (1996)	Anecdotal	**Quantitative restrictions:** manipulated distribution practices for citrus, poultry, rice, and other agricultural goods and foodstuffs. **Import clearance:** agricultural product clearance times of 2 to 4 weeks (compared with 3 to 4 days elsewhere in Asia), burdensome and sudden changes, and requirements governing labeling that can disrupt contract fulfillment. **Standards, testing, and certification:** arbitrary application of sanitary and phytosanitary standards on popcorn, apples, pears, stone fruit, beef and pork, sterilized milk products, and bottled water; cosmetic producers subjected to excessive testing and required to give confidential data to Korean industry associations with whom they compete; discriminatory testing procedures applied to foreign makers of industrial products, medical equipment, veterinary instruments, and other products. **Government procurement:** artificial disadvantages for foreign firms in construction, computers, military equipment, telecom equipment and services, power equipment, petroleum development sector, and chemicals. **Intellectual property rights (IPRs):** numerous sectors complain about inadequate attention to their IPR needs, including software firms and audiovisual and pharmaceutical companies. **Service sectors:** restrictions on participation by foreign insurance, banking, and securities firms; foreign content limitations on audiovisual material. **Investment barriers to doing business:** "Foreign investors' effective access to the Korean market continues to be conditioned under law and regulation, as well as administrative guidance and practices that are opaque and subject to variable interpretation." **Anticompetitive practices:** restricted access by foreign firms to advertising media; unfair behavior by collusive industry associations, notably in cosmetics and insurance; aggressive visible and nonvisible NTBs facing the automobile sector, including threats of tax audits for purchasers of foreign vehicles. **"Doing business" issues:** threats by government personnel to create "bad press" for foreign firms if they take complaints to their governments for redress.
PECC (1995)	Frequency ratios for "core NTBs," based on UNCTAD data base	Korean "core NTBs" used for calculation of frequency ratios in the APEC report: global quotas, antidumping investigations, duties, price undertakings. Sectors appearing to receive greatest NTB protection: agriculture and fishing, coal mining, salt mining, food processing, beverage and alcoholic beverage production, and manufacture of cement, lime, and plaster. Generally, the frequency analysis APEC conducted for Korea found a low 1.7 percent of all Korean tradeables were subject to significant NTBs.

Table. 1.1 (continued)

Source	Basis	Allegation
MITI (1996)	Anecdotal	Reported selective import bans covering 162 items (at the HS 10-digit level), including some automobiles, under Import Source Diversification System.
Yoo et al. (1993)	Unit price differentials	Found effective rate of protection for all tradeables to be on average 38.6 percent, against nominal protection of 30 percent. Based on a comparison of domestic shipment prices and foreign import prices, from extensive questionnaire responses collected from domestic firms.
Hoekman (1995)	Estimate of tariff-equivalent barriers based on "unbound" practices	Calculated tariff equivalents of nontariff barriers for a number of service sectors ranged from 16 to 185 percent at the one-digit ISIC level for classifying service activities. Particularly high tariff-equivalent rates of protection were found for maritime cabotage, postal services including courier, basic telecoms, life insurance (all 200 percent), and hard science R&D (100 percent). Many other service sectors were over 40 percent.

a. The material in this table is provided for information only. No calculations or original estimates of Korean nontariff barriers have been done by the author for this table.

Third, for the purpose of analytic simplification, a partial equilibrium model is used to estimate the static effects of protection in individual sectors.[3] A computable general equilibrium model would better capture the economywide effects of protection. However, it is a complicated task to build a computable general equilibrium model. Moreover, a general equilibrium model "diffuses" any incorrect information from one sector throughout the entire model. For these reasons, a partial equilibrium model was used.

The fourth important limitation (which relates to the preceding point) is that my calculations of the total impact of Korean protection should be understood as the arithmetic sum of individual, visible measures that restrict trade in highly protected sectors. The interactions between protection in different sectors are not examined, since that task would require a general equilibrium model. For example, the study accounts for the benefits that truck purchasers would enjoy from paying lower tariffs for imported trucks, but not the downstream benefit reflected in the lower prices that domestic food processors might charge because of lower fleet costs.

Key Findings Regarding Visible Protection Costs

Korean protection has been significantly reduced since the late 1970s, through continuous tariff cuts and the liberalization of quantitative restric-

---

3. Here is another way of describing the partial equilibrium calculations: they are conventional, elasticity-based calculations, which assume product differentiation.

tions. However, many agricultural goods and industrial products are still highly protected. The effect of Korea's remaining visible trade barriers was examined in 49 highly protected products or sectors.

The calculations indicate that consumer welfare and efficiency losses—from visible barriers alone—are significant. In 1992, the total loss in consumer surplus in the 49 products was estimated in a range between 9.2 trillion and 10.4 trillion won. This constitutes between 3.8 and 4.3 percent of Korea's GNP in 1992 and implies that each person in Korea paid 210,000 to 239,000 won in 1992 more to purchase the protected products than would have been paid with complete elimination of visible barriers. About 65 to 76 percent of the consumer surplus loss attributable to protection was transferred to domestic producers, increasing producer surplus by 6.5 trillion to 7.0 trillion won. The government collected approximately 0.4 trillion won in tariff revenues. Protection also created quota rents of around 1.0 trillion won, which were transferred to public organizations and associations handling the approval and distribution of import quotas. Most of the quota rents were eventually paid over to domestic producers, thereby augmenting the gains that the producers already enjoyed from higher domestic prices.

The remaining loss in consumer surplus, after subtracting producer surplus gain, tariff revenues, and quota rents, can be interpreted as a deadweight economic efficiency cost. This net efficiency loss is estimated to be between 0.8 trillion and 2.5 trillion won, equivalent to about 0.3 to 1.0 percent of Korea's GNP in 1992. In sum, just in terms of visible barriers, consumers finance higher incomes for producers and the government to a significant degree. In addition, protection creates a loss in economic efficiency.

When trade is completely liberalized, standard theory tells us that there will be an increase in imports. According to the calculations made here, the Korean economy would experience an increase in imports of between 2.9 trillion and 10.9 trillion won ($3.7 billion to $14.0 billion) if visible trade barriers were completely abolished in the 49 products examined in the report. This calculation implies that Korea's potential imports for the products in question would have expanded by 94 to 350 percent over the actual imports realized for those products in 1992.

Liberalization of imports would also boost exports, through a combination of microeconomic and macroeconomic effects. In terms of microeconomic impacts, cheaper imports would reduce the raw material and intermediate input costs of export industries and would moderate their wage costs. Wage costs would be reduced because workers would be released from import-competing industries and because a monthly wage denominated in a certain number of won would buy more goods and services. At a macroeconomic level, there could be some depreciation of the won in foreign exchange markets, and this too would boost exports.

Trade liberalization of the 49 products would reduce their domestic production, mainly because it would cause prices to fall and the volume of imports to rise. With elimination of visible barriers, it is estimated that domestic production would decline by approximately 2.2 trillion to 5.2 trillion won, which is equivalent to 5 to 12 percent of the actual output of the affected goods in 1992. The decline in output would cause a loss of jobs in the affected industries. Estimates made here indicate that 174,000 to 405,000 workers would have been dislocated if the government had completely abolished visible protection on these products in 1992. This accounts for 8 to 19 percent of actual employment in the affected sectors in 1992.

Sectoral Comparison and Evaluation

As expected, the largest impact of liberalization occurs in the agriculture and fishery sector, which accounts for 50 to 70 percent of the total impact in terms of consumer and producer welfare, as well as imports and production, and for more than 90 percent of the employment effect.

Elimination of visible barriers would have the next largest impact on the food-processing sector, including dairy products. This sector accounts for some 14 to 19 percent of the various effects, except for employment. The employment effect for this industry is estimated to be only 2 percent of the total employment impact, reflecting a high capital-to-labor ratio in food processing.

The food-processing sector is followed by the machinery and metal sector, which accounts for 7 to 14 percent of the total impact on consumer and producer surplus, imports, and production. As with food processing, the effect on employment is relatively low, at around 1 percent of the total employment effect.

The light industry sector, including textiles, accounts for 5 to 18 percent of total consumer welfare, import, and production effects, and 3 to 4 percent of total employment effects.

The cost of protection in the agriculture and fishery sector, as measured by the loss of consumer surplus, is largely offset—at least in the public mind—by the direct benefit of protection, namely maintaining existing employment. Out of the total increase in consumer surplus due to trade liberalization, 72 to 73 percent can be attributed to the agriculture and fishery sector. At the same time, virtually all the reduction in employment comes from this sector, accounting for 92 to 93 percent of the reduction. Rice is the outstanding example of a disproportionate relationship between consumer gains and employment losses.[4] While 35 to 38 percent

---

4. Employment loss would be accompanied by a drop in farm income and eventual, if slow, migration from rural to urban areas.

of the total gain in consumer surplus originates in the rice sector, more than 60 percent of the total reduction in employment can be attributed to rice.

Most urban residents now living in Seoul, Pusan, and other large cities were raised in farming areas. Accordingly, they sympathize with rural people. These sympathies go far to explain Korea's insistence on a very gradual pace of market liberalization for major agricultural items, especially rice.

Organization of the Remainder of the Study

Chapter 2 of the report provides an overview of the recent trend of trade liberalization in Korea. It surveys protection on selected products, using 1992 data.

In chapter 3, various effects of protection are estimated for highly protected sectors. Key magnitudes are identified, including changes in consumer and producer surplus, government revenues, imports, domestic production, and the level of employment. Chapter 3 concludes by comparing the results of former studies of Korean protection and the results derived here. It also contrasts the outcomes of similar studies of the costs of protection in the United States, Japan, and Korea. Finally, the chapter summarizes the study, draws some conclusions on limitations of the research approach, and makes proposals for the direction of future studies.

Appendix A describes the methodology for calculating the costs of protection, and the likely effects of liberalization, by sector; the tables in appendix B provide base-year data and the results in tabular form, sector by sector.

2

Trade Protection in Korea

The first section in this chapter presents an overview of trade liberalization in Korea, along with some indices. The second section evaluates, on an industry-by-industry basis, the background of protective measures and the future prospects of liberalization. In the third section, highly protected products are identified, and their protection levels are measured, based on 1992 data. This last section also summarizes the characteristics of these products and sectors.

Recent Trends in Trade Liberalization

Import Liberalization

In Korea's early stages of industrialization during the 1960s, imports were severely restricted as a way of curbing chronic trade deficits. In the 1970s, import restrictions were continued, while Korea focused primarily on developing heavy and chemical industries. It was not until the late 1970s that the Korean government promoted competition and market opening as a way to improve the efficiency of the Korean economy. Since then, the government has steadily liberalized import restrictions.

Korea's trading system is regulated under the Foreign Trade Act and the Customs Act. The goals of these acts are both to promote external trade and to maintain orderly and fair trading practices consistent with international trading rules. As a result, Korea can only regulate imports consistent with international trade norms or agreements, or in order to

Table 2.1   Import liberalization ratio for Korean imports, 1983-97

Year	Total (A)	Number of items[a] Subject to automatic import approval (B)	Under import restrictions	Import liberalization ratio (B/A × 100)	Number of items under import source diversification system
1983	7,560	6,078	1,482	80.4	644
1984	7,915	6,712	1,203	84.8	591
1985	7,915	6,944	971	87.7	461
1986	7,915	7,252	663	91.6	413
1987	7,915	7,426	489	93.8	381
1988	7,915	7,553	362	95.4	344
1989	10,241	9,776	465	95.5	262
1990	10,274	9,898	376	96.3	268
1991	10,274	9,991	283	97.2	258
1992	10,322	10,080	242	97.7	258
1993	10,417	10,221	196	98.1	255
1994	10,502	10,352	150	98.6	230
1995	10,859	10,744	115	98.9	187
1996	10,859	10,778	81	99.3	162
1997	10,859	10,851	8	99.9	n.a.

a. Items are identified by 8-digit CCCN (Customs Cooperation Council Nomenclature) for 1983-88 and by 10-digit HS (Harmonized System of Commodity Description) for 1989-97.

Source: Korean Ministry of Trade, Industry, and Energy.

Table 2.2   Import liberalization ratio for Korean imports of agricultural products, 1989-97

Year	Total	Number of items[a] Subject to automatic import approval	Under import restrictions	Import liberalization ratio
1989	1,790	1,364	426	76.2
1990	1,790	1,439	351	80.4
1991	1,790	1,517	273	84.7
1992	1,790	1,560	230	87.2
1993	1,790	1,604	186	89.6
1994	1,790	1,648	142	92.1
1995	2,022	1,916	106	94.8
1996	2,022	1,950	72	96.4
1997	2,022	2,014	8	99.6

a. Items are identified by their 8-digit CCCN (Customs Cooperation Council Nomenclature) for 1983-88 and by their 10-digit HS (Harmonized System of the Commodity Description) for 1989-94.

Source: Korean Ministry of Trade, Industry, and Energy.

preserve fair trade. Under the Foreign Trade Act, imports and exports are regulated under a system of "Export-Import Public Notices" and "Consolidated Public Notices."

Export-Import Public Notices may be tabulated to measure an "import liberalization ratio" (tables 2.1 and 2.2). The ratio is defined as the percentage of total tariff lines in which imports are automatically approved by authorized foreign exchange banks upon submission of the required documents. The ratio was 80 percent in 1983 and rose to 99 percent in 1995. A higher ratio can be interpreted as indicating a less restrictive use of a major form of Korean nontariff barrier. In 1995, imports of 115 items, from a total of 10,859 tariff lines listed at the 10-digit level under the Harmonized System (HS) of Commodity Description, were still subject to some restrictions.[1] Almost all the 115 items are agricultural products. Imports of nearly all manufactured goods, on the other hand, are automatically approved.

Besides the export-import notification system under the Foreign Trade Act, Korea's exports and imports of some items are regulated by the Consolidated Public Notices system, which compiles individual laws for transparency and for the convenience of affected parties. These individual laws include the Fisheries Act, the Ginseng and Tobacco Business Act, the Foodgrain Control Act, the Pharmaceuticals Act, and the Industrial Goods Quality Control Act, to mention some important examples. They impose conditions and procedures for the export and import of the specified products. Agricultural and marine products, livestock, and their processed goods account for most of these regulated products, followed by medical supplies and a few other manufactured goods.

In addition, in 1994 the importation of some 230 Japanese products (again 10-digit HS items) was restricted through the "import source diversification system." Under Article 25, clauses 3 and 4 of the Enforcement Ordinance of the Foreign Trade Act, Korea may control imports from a country with which Korea has a severe and chronic trade deficit. Such a country is defined as one whose ratio of trade surplus with Korea to the bilateral trade volume was among the highest observed during the past five years. Under Article 25, the government may identify products that are to be imported from countries other than Japan. These are called "import source diversification products." A list of these products is publicly announced and administered separately from other items under the public notices.

The procedure for selecting import source diversification products is as follows. First, businesses in the private sector and related associations offer recommendations to the government. After discussions within the Ministry of Trade, Industry, and Energy, the minister finalizes the list of products. Certain factors are given special weight in drawing up the list. The list emphasizes products that have a substantial effect both on correcting the bilateral trade imbalance with the country in question and on diversifying import sources, products that have been imported in large amounts for domestic consumption or whose importation is expected to surge, and products made by domestic infant industries.

---

1. The term "Harmonized System" refers to the multilaterally agreed system of tariff classification.

The diversification system does not abide by the principle of nondiscrimination. In light of this complaint, the Korean government plans to reduce the number of items under the system and eventually abolish it. In fact, by 1996 the number of Japanese products effectively banned at the 10-digit HS level had been reduced from 230 to 162.

Tariffs

Since the 1960s, when Korea adopted a set of outward-oriented economic policies, it has continued its tariff reforms. One highlight is that since 1983, Korea has twice implemented five-year tariff reduction programs. The objective of tariff reform has been to increase the competitiveness of industries both by lowering peak tariff rates, thereby narrowing the dispersion of rates, and by improving the predictability and transparency of the tariff system.

A tariff reform program was implemented between 1984 and 1988 as part of a comprehensive economic liberalization package. Besides lowering tariff rates, the package aimed at reducing the industry-specific use of tariff abatements as a tool of industrial policy. Under the program, the average tariff was lowered to 18.1 percent and tariff dispersion was substantially narrowed. The collected tariff rates for product categories presented in this study were calculated as realized tariff revenue divided by the combined c.i.f. import values[2] of underlying tariff line items. The collected tariff rates were calculated from data on imports and tariff revenue kept on magnetic tape by the Korea Customs Service and the Korea Customs Research Institute.

In 1988, a new five-year tariff reduction program was introduced covering 1989 to 1993. In 1990, its staged implementation was deferred by one year to offset losses in fiscal revenue resulting from the elimination of the defense tax. By 1994, the unweighted average tariff rate for all product categories had been reduced to 7.9 percent, slightly higher than the average in advanced countries such as the United States, Japan, and the European Union and significantly lower than the average tariff level of most developing countries.

In 1992, Korea had a tariff abatement system to refund duties paid on imported inputs that were subsequently reexported as part of finished goods. This rebate system applied to certain goods, such as high-technology products not manufactured domestically, machinery for defense industries, and some other inputs. However, imports of these items were not very large. Therefore, the duty remission system did not appear to play a major role in creating the spread between "statutory" and "collected" tariff rates, but it nevertheless was taken into account in this

---

2. That is, the system of valuing imports by cost, insurance, and freight.

Table 2.3 Average Korean tariff rates, 1983-94
         (percent)

Year	Average tariff rates on imports of:		
	Manufactures	Agricultural products	Total
1983	22.6	31.4	23.7
1984	20.6	29.6	21.9
1985	20.3	28.8	21.3
1986	18.7	27.1	19.9
1987	18.2	26.4	19.3
1988	16.9	25.2	18.1
1989	11.2	20.6	12.7
1990	9.7	19.9	11.4
1991	9.7	19.9	11.4
1992	8.4	18.5	10.1
1993	7.1	17.8	8.9
1994	6.2	16.6	7.9

Source: Korean Ministry of Finance.

study. There also existed a tariff refund system in 1992, which worked by returning import tariffs paid for intermediate goods going into subsequently exported goods (similar to a duty drawback). This study did not take into account the tariff refund on imported inputs for exported goods in calculating the collected tariff rates.

To summarize: during the 11 years following 1983, Korea cut its tariff rates substantially. The average tariff rate on manufactured goods was reduced from 22.6 percent in 1983 to 6.2 percent in 1994. By 1994, tariffs no longer played an important role in protecting the manufacturing sector as a whole (table 2.3).

The average tariff on agricultural goods was also reduced, but at a slower pace, from 31.4 percent in 1983 to 16.6 percent in 1994. This reflected the fragile structure of Korea's agricultural sector, the lengthy period required for the migration of rural people to urban areas, and political sensitivity to the interests of the agricultural sector. (For tariff rates of agricultural items on a two-digit HS basis, see appendix table A.1.)

Before 1983, Korea maintained a steep tariff escalation system in which rates levied on final products were higher than those levied on intermediate goods, which, in turn, were higher than those on raw materials. Such systems were, and still are, common among developing countries. Tariff escalation provides more protection for the later stages of manufacturing and less for intermediate goods and raw materials. Some observers pointed out that this could lead to excessive consumption of raw industrial materials and could unduly bias the industrial structure toward assembly and processing activities. Reflecting these criticisms, after 1983 the degree of tariff escalation was reduced substantially for most products, as part of the general tariff reduction program.

Table 2.4 gives the estimates of Yoo et al. (1993) for effective and nominal rates of protection for several sectors in the year 1990. Yoo et al.'s estimates

Table 2.4 Effective and nominal rates of protection for selected sectors, 1990: Yoo et al.'s estimates

Industry	Effective rate of protection[a]	Nominal rate of protection[b]
Agriculture	159.7	101.9
Rice	499.6	311.0
Vegetables	13.1	15.4
Fruits	140.1	98.8
Livestock	144.3	43.5
Forestry	6.4	7.5
Fisheries	15.0	13.9
Mining	−2.1	0.4
Manufacturing except foods	20.2	13.9
Plywood	5.3	6.4
Wooden furniture	−2.3	4.2
Textiles	−8.5	5.2
Apparel	71.0	29.7
Industrial chemicals	13.6	11.3
Other chemicals	49.4	29.0
Glass and glassware	11.1	10.7
Ceramic products	6.2	7.7
Metallic household articles	18.7	12.9
Other metallic articles	29.0	16.0
General machinery	25.0	17.3
Electrical machinery	77.5	35.4
Transportation machinery	13.0	13.6
Automobiles	16.6	14.8
Total tradeables	38.6	30.0
Tradeables except agriculture	19.7	22.5

a. The effective rate of protection for sector j is defined as $[VA_j/VA_j^* − 1]$, where VA_j is value added at domestic prices for inputs and outputs, and VA_j^* is value added at world prices.
b. For most industrial products, the nominal rate of protection corresponds to the difference between domestic prices and border prices obtained from price survey data. For agricultural, forestry, and fishery products, the nominal rates refer to tariffs plus the tariff equivalent of nontariff barriers.

Source: Yoo et al. 1993, 142-45 (table VI-1), 177 (table VII-1).

of nominal rates of protection were based on a large-scale survey, carried out in 1992, of shipment prices of domestic goods and import prices for competing foreign goods. These estimated nominal rates should in principle reflect nontariff barriers as well as tariffs. In fact, the results of Yoo et al.'s survey suggest a nontariff barrier tariff equivalent of about 11 percent for tradeables except agriculture, above and beyond the known tariff average of 11 percent in 1990.

In recent years, the Korean government has steadily shifted the tariff structure toward a uniform rate system under which, in principle, a single rate is levied on all products. To the extent this goal is achieved, the tariff is neutralized as a factor affecting competitive conditions among Korean industries. The modal or central tariff rate was lowered in 1994 to 8 percent from 20 percent in 1988. In 1994, items with tariff rates below 10 percent reached 93.4 percent of the total (table 2.5).

Table 2.5 Structure of Korea's tariff rates, 1984-94 (percent)

			Percent of tariff lines			
Year	Simple average rate	Central rate[a]	Under 10 percent	10-20 percent	20 percent	Over 20 percent
1984	21.9	n.a.	24.2	5.5	41.9	28.4
1988	18.1	20	25.8	4.3	61.8	8.1
1990	11.4	13	40.2	53.0	1.5	5.3
1992	10.1	11	40.7	53.6	1.4	5.3
1994	7.9	8	93.4	0	1.4	5.2

n.a. = not available
a. "Central rate" or "modal rate" means the most frequent tariff rate for that year.
Source: Korean Ministry of Finance.

Korea plans to reduce and even abolish some tariffs within the next few years, in accordance with the zero-for-zero tariff reduction plan agreed in the Uruguay Round negotiations. Under zero-for-zero rate schemes on manufactured goods, tariffs will gradually be lowered and eventually removed over the next 8 to 15 years from some 126 items in the following sectors: iron and steel, construction equipment, farming machinery, medical equipment, furniture, medical supplies, electronics (including semiconductors), paper, toys, and nonferrous metals. Under harmonization schemes of tariff reduction in the chemical products category, the rates of 193 items identified by four-digit HS codes will be substantially lowered to between zero and 6.5 percent within the next 5 to 10 years.

In principle, the tariff rates applied to imported goods are set in the tariff schedule annexed to the Customs Act. The act also provides for a flexible tariff system, designed to cope with short-term problems in the economic circumstances of individual industries. Under this system, the government can temporarily raise or lower tariffs under certain conditions. The flexible tariff rates defined in the Customs Act are antidumping duties (Article 10), emergency tariffs (Article 12), adjustment tariffs (Article 12, clause 2), countervailing duties (Article 13), and tariff quotas (Article 16).

Among these, antidumping duties, emergency tariffs, adjustment tariffs, countervailing duties, and some tariff quotas are used to control imports by raising tariff rates. However, in other cases, tariff quotas are used to push tariff rates below the statutory rate for a defined volume of imports, so as to encourage imports and stabilize the domestic price of specific items. (For a list of products with flexible tariffs above the statutory rates, and their specific rates and periods, see appendix tables A.2-A.5.)

Trade Protection by Sector

This section estimates protection levels by individual product, examining for each sector the main components of trade protection, its background and history, and future liberalization schedules.

Table 2.6 Importance of the agricultural sector in the Korean economy, 1980-93

	1980	1985	1990	1993
Output (trillions of won)	5.7	10.2	15.6	18.8
Percent share of GNP	15.4	12.9	8.7	7.1
Employment (millions of workers)	4.7	3.7	3.3	3.0
Percent share of total employment	34.1	24.9	18.3	16.0
Imports (billions of dollars)	3.3	3.2	6.8	7.4
Percent share of total imports	14.8	10.3	9.8	8.8
Trade balance (billions of dollars)	−1.9	−1.8	−4.3	−4.9

Source: Korean National Statistical Office 1995.

Agricultural Products

Economic activity in agriculture (including fisheries and livestock) has sharply declined as a share of GDP ever since Korea adopted an outward-oriented development strategy in the early 1960s. Faced with this decline, Korea has maintained policies to support domestic prices and restrain imports of foreign foodgrains and livestock. Foodgrains and livestock are important sources of livelihood for most farmers in terms both of their diet and income, and they also further national goals of promoting self-sufficiency in the supply of major food items and of reducing the earnings gap between rural and urban households.

But the costs of agricultural support, specifically the associated rise in land prices and mounting international pressures since the mid-1980s for food import liberalization, have begun to shift Korea's trade policy on agricultural imports. Agricultural tariffs have been reduced, the wheat market was opened somewhat in 1984, the beef market is gradually being opened, and structural adjustment in agriculture is being pursued under the Rural Development Act of 1990.

The share of agriculture in real GDP fell from 45 percent in 1963 to 25 percent in the early 1970s, then to about 15 percent in 1980, and even further to about 7 percent in the 1990s. Concurrently, the percentage of the labor force employed in the agricultural sector declined from just over 60 percent in the early 1960s to 30 percent in the 1980s and then to 16 percent in the early 1990s. With agricultural imports increasing rapidly to $7.4 billion in 1993, the trade deficit in this sector amounted to $4.9 billion in that year (table 2.6).

High Tariffs and Flexible Tariff Systems

Even though average tariffs on agriculture products (including fisheries and livestock) and processed foods have been lowered during the second five-year tariff reduction schedules commencing in 1989, certain major crops, and their processed goods, continue to be protected by relatively

Table 2.7 Composition of tariff rates in major agricultural products, 1994

Tariff rates (percent)	Major items	Number of items	Percent shares of total items
50+	Onions, garlic, peppers, apples, chestnut, pork	38	8.7
40-50	Peanuts, sesame, tea, milk, cheese, butter, whiskey, wine	23	5.3
30-40	Beef, potatoes, bananas, almonds, alcohols, malt	72	16.5
25-30	Sunflower seeds and sunflower oil	7	1.6
20-25	Antlers, fresh or chilled fish, crustaceans, manioc chips, ginseng, leaf tobacco	38	8.7
10-20	Live or frozen fish, cuttlefish	6	1.4
0-8	Seeds, rice, barley, corn, coffee, cocoa	252	57.8
Total		436	100.0

Source: Tariff Schedule annexed to the Customs Act of Korea.

Table 2.8 Agricultural products under the flexible tariff system

Type of tariff	Products (HS)	Tariff rates (percent)	Period
Adjustment tariff	Chinese vermicelli (1902)	60	1/92-12/94
	Carrots (0706), oak mushroom and bracken (1709-0712), persimmons (0813), tropical fish (0301), bai top shell (1605), acorns (2308)	100	1/93-12/94
	Maejoo and mixed seasonings (2103), acorn flours (2106)	60	1/93-12/94
	Sugar confectionery (1704), chocolate preparations (1806)	75	1/93-12/94
Emergency tariff	Pork in airtight containers (1602)	40	7/91-6/93
Tariff quota	Soybean oil (1507)	25	6/91-6/93
	Bananas (0803)	90	1/92-12/93

Source: Korean Ministry of Finance.

high tariff rates. Some 38 tariff line items had tariffs of 50 percent or more in 1994, and items with a tariff above 20 percent constituted about 41 percent of all agricultural tariff lines (table 2.7).

On the other hand, so-called flexible tariff systems, such as the emergency tariff, adjustment tariff, and tariff quotas, were sometimes used to shield domestic producers from injury due to import surges of agricultural goods and processed foods. Higher rates under the flexible tariff system were applied to pork in airtight containers, soybean oil, bananas, and Chinese vermicelli in 1992, and to other items such as carrots and oak mushrooms in 1993 (table 2.8).

Import Approval Procedures and Quotas

Trade protection of agriculture is also maintained through import approval procedures and the import recommendation system managed by the Export-Import Public Notice and the Consolidated Public Notice systems (appendix tables A.6 and A.7). Also, price stabilization schemes for cereals, livestock and their by-products, and a range of vegetables and seasoning items are administered either directly by the government or by public or semipublic organizations, including the National Agricultural Cooperative Federation, the Agricultural and Fisheries Marketing Corporation, the National Livestock Cooperative Federation, the Livestock Product Marketing Organization, the Korea Ocean Fisheries Association, and the Korea Milk Processing Industry Association.

Under special laws regulating agricultural imports, specified items can be imported only if the respective government authorities or related organizations approve an import license. Above all, via the Foodgrain Control Act, the government maintains purchasing control over major food products (rice and barley) in order to stabilize their prices and support the income of farmers. Imports of corn, potatoes, and starch need approval from the National Agricultural Cooperative Federation, while soybeans, red beans, and green beans need approval from the Agricultural and Fisheries Marketing Corporation. Under the Animal Feed Control Act, imports of feed grains need the recommendation of the Korea Foods Industry Association, except corn used for feed, which needs approval from the National Livestock Cooperative Federation. Under the Ginseng and the Tobacco Business Acts, exports and imports of ginseng, tobacco, and related goods can be regulated by the Korea Tobacco and Ginseng Corporation to promote fair trade and the industrial development of ginseng and tobacco.[3]

Although the tariff equivalents of nontariff barriers differ according to calculation methods and available data, table 2.9 shows the tariff equivalents of major agricultural products according to the sources that are used in this study.

Domestic Production and Imports

Korea is currently self-sufficient in rice and barley for food consumption and, until 1994, did not import either product (table 2.10). These two items comprise 90 percent of total grain production in Korea. The tariff rates on edible rice and barley are only 5 percent, but price stabilization schemes and implicit zero import quotas effectively translate into much higher tariff-equivalent barriers—above 300 percent. However, domesti-

---

3. Ginseng is a perennial herb whose roots are used as a drug, as a stimulating tea, and as a source of aromatic bitters. Korean ginseng products offered by the corporation are highly prized in some markets.

Table 2.9 Tariff equivalents of major agricultural products

	Items	Tariff equivalents
Tariffication of the Uruguay Round	Raw barley	333.0
	Beer barley	570.0
	Corn	365.0
	Soybeans	541.0
	Peanuts	256.1
	Potatoes	338.0
	Sweet potatoes	428.0
	Green beans	675.0
	Red beans	467.5
	Manioc	986.0
	Ginseng and products	247.6-838.1
Ceiling binding of the Uruguay Round	Peppers	300.0
	Garlics	400.0
	Onions	150.0
	Sesame	700.0
	Powdered milk	220.0
	Concentrated milk	99.0
	Malt	299.0
Other items	Chestnuts	243.8
	Walnuts	50.0
	Pine nuts	629.8
	Ginkgo	30.0
	Jujubes	679.4
	Green tea	570.7
	Mandarin oranges	160.0
Major items under restriction	Rice	595.0
	Beef	169.0
	Pork	51.0
	Chicken	65.0

Sources: Korea's Economic Planning Board 1992; Uruguay Round Schedule LX 1994.

cally consumed wheat and corn are mostly imported, and imports of soybeans are increasing rapidly.

In the case of livestock, imports have been restrained largely through price stabilization schemes, import authorization procedures, and import quotas. The beef import quota, administered by the Livestock Product Marketing Organization, has been raised progressively from 15,000 metric tons in 1988 to 115,000 tons in 1991. Imports in 1991 were somewhat exceeded by domestic output.

The price stabilization schemes for pork and chicken are administered by the National Livestock Cooperative Federation, with imports authorized by the federation when domestic market prices exceed the upper limit of the price stabilization band. In the case of chicken, there were no imports between 1987 and 1991. The tariffs on milk, butter, and cheese amount to 40 percent, and imports of these dairy products accounted for only 1.4 percent of total domestic consumption in 1992. Table 2.10 summarizes the self-sufficiency ratios for major agricultural goods since

Table 2.10 Self-sufficiency ratio of major agricultural products

Product	1970-74	1980-84	1990	1992
Rice	89	88	108	98
Barley	90	100	96	83
Corn	15	4	2	2
Soybean	81	29	20	12
Beef	94	67	53	44
Pork	102	100	101	103
Poultry meat	100	100	100	100

Sources: GATT 1992; Korea Rural Economic Institute 1993.

1974. For beef and for feed grains, imports have substantially increased; for other goods, imports are still severely restricted.

Import Liberalization Schedules after the Uruguay Round

In accordance with agreements made in the Uruguay Round of multilateral trade negotiations, Korea has promised to accelerate trade reform in the agricultural sector. All agricultural products, with the notable exception of rice, are now being liberalized through tariffication, ceiling bindings of tariffs, and gradual tariff reductions.[4]

For items previously subject to quantitative restriction and restrictive import-licensing under individual laws (appendix table A.6), Korea will convert the restrictions into ordinary customs duties (tariffication), starting with a base equal to the tariff equivalents of quantitative restrictions, usually measured by the differential between domestic and external prices. Tariff rates will then be reduced by 10 percent of the base tariff level over the next 10 years. For example, a tariff of 40 percent would be reduced to 36 percent, over 10 years. For items such as barley and potatoes, which recorded little or no import volume, the government will be required to permit the import of a Minimum Market Access (MMA) level, defined as 3 to 5 percent of domestic total consumption. For items whose imports were much bigger than 3 percent of domestic consumption, the government will be required to maintain Current Market Access (CMA), defined as the current level of imports.

For rice, tariffication will be deferred for 10 years under section B of Annex 5 in the WTO Agreement on Agriculture. In the meantime, Korea will permit imports with an MMA of 1 percent in 1995, growing to 4 percent by 2004. The tariffication of Korea's rice restrictions will be reviewed again in 2004.

Major import items that were traditionally subject to quantitative restraints under the Export-Import Public Notice system are being liberal-

---

4. The term "ceiling binding" refers to the maximum tariff rate that may be imposed on an item under a country's schedule filed with the GATT/WTO. The country's applied tariff may, of course, be less than the ceiling binding.

ized, but with higher tariff rates than previously applied. In other words, quantitative restrictions on these items are being removed, but the quotas are being replaced by higher tariffs. For certain so-called balance of payments (BOP) items, namely pork, chicken, and oranges, the new—and higher—tariffs will be "bound" under the GATT/WTO (i.e., Korea promises not to increase its tariffs beyond the new, higher rates). At the Balance of Payments Committee of the GATT meeting in October 1989, Korea agreed to liberalize the import market for these BOP items by July 1997. For beef, the period of quantitative restraints on imports will be prolonged to the year 2000. In 1995, the tariff rate was raised to 43.6 percent, up from its pre-Uruguay Round level of 20 percent. The tariff rate on beef will gradually be reduced from 43.6 percent in 1995 to 40 percent in 2004. At the same time, the import quota of 123,000 tons in 1995 will be raised to 225,000 tons in 2000. By this combination of policy measures, quota protection will be replaced by tariff protection, and overall there will be some liberalization of beef imports (table 2.11). After the year 2000, import quotas on beef will be completely eliminated and only tariffs will remain.

Peppers, garlic, onions, sesame, milk products, and other items that did not have bound tariffs before the Uruguay Round will be liberalized from January 1995 on, with tariff rates bound at ceiling levels no higher than the previous price differentials between domestic and external prices. Imports of less important agricultural items such as apples, grapes, and fruit juices (not listed in table 2.11), which were subject to import restrictions under the Export-Import Public Notice system, will likewise be liberalized, but in these cases starting with their pre-Uruguay Round tariff rates, beginning in January 1995 or January 1996, depending upon the item. All the tariff rates on these items will be reduced by 24 percent of the base tariff level over a 10-year period.

Mineral Products

Because Korea is poorly endowed with mineral resources, it has very low tariff rates on most minerals and primary energy sources (1 to 2 percent for mineral ore, 3 to 5 percent for stone, 1 to 5 percent for coal, and 5 percent for crude petroleum and natural gas). Although importers of anthracite coal, the only fossil fuel in Korea, are required to obtain an import recommendation from the Korea Coal Corporation, Korea maintains low import barriers on all types of coal. Imported coals constituted 68 percent of domestic consumption in 1992. Moreover, under the Petroleum Industry Act, firms can only import the amount of petroleum specified in a petroleum purchasing contract that has been approved by the Ministry of Trade, Industry, and Energy with the recommendation of the Korea Petroleum Association. The rationale for this procedure is to ensure a stable supply of petroleum.

Table 2.11 Main contents of Uruguay Round schedules for Korea's agricultural products

Items	Tariff rates (percent)			MMA/CMA amounts (thousands of tons)[a]		State trading (import mark-up)
	Existing (1994)	1995	2004	Initial year	Final year[b]	
Rice	5	0	0	51.3	205.2	Yes
Naked barley	20	333 (or 401 won/kg)	299.7 (or 361 won/kg)	14.2	23.6	Yes
Soybeans	5	541 (or 1,062 won/kg)	487 (or 956 won/kg)	1,032.2	1,032.2	Yes
Corn for feed	3	365	328	6,102.1	6,102.1	No
Potatoes	30	338	304	11.3	18.8	Yes
Sweet potatoes	20	428 (or 375 won/kg)	385 (or 338 won/kg)	11.2	18.5	Yes
Beef	20	43.6	40	123.0[c]	225.0[c]	Yes
Pork (frozen)	25	37	25	22.0[c]	18.3[c]	No
Chicken	20	35	20	7.7[c]	6.5[c]	No
Milk products (skim milk powder)	20	220	176	0.6	1.0	No
Peppers	50	300 (or 6,900 won/kg)	270 (or 6,210 won/kg)	4.3	7.2	Yes
Garlic	50	400 (or 2,000 won/kg)	360 (or 1,800 won/kg)	8.7	14.5	Yes
Onions	50	150 (or 200 won/kg)	135 (or 180 won/kg)	12.4	20.7	Yes
Oranges	50	99	50	15.0	57.0	Yes
Sesame oil	40	700 (or 7,400 won/kg)	630 (or 6,600 won/kg)	6.7	6.7	Yes

a. For imports within Minimum Market Access (MMA) or Current Market Access (CMA) amounts, existing tariff rates shall be applied.
b. The final year is 2004, with exceptions of beef (2000), pork (January–June 1997), and chicken (January–June 1997).
c. These are import quotas.

Sources: Korean Ministry of Agriculture, Forestry, and Fisheries 1994; *Uruguay Round Schedule LX* 1994.

Table 2.12 Chemical products under the flexible tariff system

Type of tariff	Items (HSK)	Target countries	Tariff rates (percent)	Period
Adjustment tariff	Films of plastics (3920)	All partners	30.0	1/93-12/94
Emergency tariff	Polyethylene film (390210)	All partners	25.0	10/90-9/92
Antidumping duties[a]	Polyacetals (3907.10.0000)	US, Japan	4.0	9/91-9/93
	Phosphoric acid (2809.20.1000)	China	44.7-59.3 40.9-54.3	10/92-2/93 2/93-2/96
	Photographic plates for graphic art (3701)	Japan	24.5-28.7	11/93-11/98
	Sodium ash (2836.20.0000)	China	66.1	1/94-1/97

a. Antidumping duties are levied in addition to the basic tariff rates.
Source: Korean Ministry of Finance.

Among minerals, natural steatite had the highest tariff: a rate of 30 percent imposed from July 1991 to June 1993. This was a temporary measure to protect the domestic steatite producers, who suffered from a sudden increase in imports of natural steatite used as a paper filler and as an additive in cosmetics and paint. In late 1993, the tariff rate was restored to the statutory level of 5 percent.

Although the tariff rates of mineral products have ranged from zero to 8 percent since 1994, the average collected tariff rate was around 1 percent in 1994, inasmuch as statutory rates of 1 to 2 percent were applied to most items.

Chemical Products

During 1992, the statutory tariff rates on chemical products had relatively low levels—zero on some pharmaceutical products and up to 11 percent on most others. There were some exceptions. The rates on perfumes, makeup ingredients, oral hygiene product ingredients, and shaving ingredients (HS 3303 through 3307) were 13 percent, and on casein (a protein material derived from milk) the tariff was 20 percent, the highest rate imposed on any chemical product.

Apart from tariffs, which are generally low, other restrictive mechanisms were used to limit chemical imports. Table 2.12 lists the chemical products subject to moderately high temporary tariffs (roughly 25 to 60 percent), as well as the length of time each item remained under the flexible tariff system.

Some protection arises from import licensing procedures applied for various health, safety, and environmental reasons. First, food-related chemicals, such as ethyl acetate (HS 2915.31), which is used as a food additive, must meet technical standards and undergo a quarantine procedure when imported under the Food Sanitation Act. Second, for some pharmaceutical products, such as vitamins (HS 2936.10), the recommendation of the Korea Pharmaceutical Industry Association may be required pursuant to the Pharmaceuticals Act. These recommendations are supposed to reflect health and safety considerations. Likewise, imports of some quasi-pharmaceuticals in cosmetics need to be approved by the Ministry of Health and Social Welfare, under the Pharmaceuticals Act. Third, certain chemical products, such as acrylonitrile (HS 2926.10), must be registered with the Ministry of Environment prior to importation, under the Toxic Chemical Act. Fourth, for the import of most fertilizers, the recommendation of the Ministry of Agriculture, Fishing, and Forestry or of the Korea Fertilizer Industry Association is required under the Fertilizer Management Act.

Not only were the tariff rates on chemical products reduced to an average of 8 percent by 1994, but additional reductions will occur in the future. Korea participated in the harmonization schemes for tariff reduction in the Uruguay Round and agreed to reduce the rates of 193 chemical products (defined as HS four-digit items) to levels of less than 6.5 percent.

Wood and Paper

With few forests, Korea relies on imports for more than 80 percent of raw materials such as logs, lumber, and pulp. Low tariff rates of 2 to 8 percent are imposed on the import of most wood and paper products, and a zero rate is placed on most publications and printed materials.

However, higher tariffs have been applied from time to time on selected processed products. Using the flexible tariff system, the rate on wooden chopsticks was 53 percent between April 1991 and December 1994, on plywood 15 percent (January 1992-December 1994), and on veneer sheets and rounded wooden bars 51 percent (January 1993-December 1994). Appendix table A.2 gives more details.

Textiles and Clothing

As a major exporting industry with a large number of workers, the textile and clothing industry once played an important role in the rapid growth of the Korean economy. Even in 1990, this industry still made up about 20 percent of total exports and 20 percent of employment in manufacturing activities (table 2.13). Although no special statute was enacted to protect the domestic industry, there was obvious tariff escalation: higher tariff rates were imposed on items with a higher degree of processing. This

Table 2.13 Importance of the textile industry in the Korean economy[a]

Economic indicator	Year	Amount	Percentage share of Korean economy[b]
Exports	1993	US$16 billion	19.4
Imports	1993	US$ 4 billion	4.9
Output	1992	$28 billion[c]	9.7
Value added	1992	$13 billion[c]	10.6
Employment	1992	522,000 workers	18.6

a. The textile industry covers sectors of Korea Standard Industrial Classification (KSIC) 17 and 18.
b. For exports and imports, the percent shares are measured as shares of Korean exports and imports. For other indicators, the shares are measured as shares of Korean manufactures.
c. Based on the 1992 average exchange rate of 781 won = $1.
Sources: Korean National Statistical Office 1994; Korean Ministry of Finance 1994.

Table 2.14 Textile products subject to adjustment tariffs

Items (HS)	Tariff rates (percent)	Period
Mats (4601)	100	1/93-12/94
Raw silk (5002)	50	1/94-12/94
Woven wool fabrics (5111-5112)	19	1/94-12/94
Woven cotton fabrics (5208)	40	1/93-12/94
Woven fabrics of synthetic staple fibers (5515)	19	1/94-12/94
Cotton gauze (5803)	40	1/93-12/94
Cotton gloves (6116)	60/40[a]	1/93-12/94
Cotton toilet and kitchen linen (6302)	75/50[a]	1/93-12/94

a. Numbers after slashes correspond to the tariff rates applied in 1994.
Source: Korean Ministry of Finance.

was an important reason why the import of apparel was insignificant compared with the import of raw materials and yarn.

In 1992, the tariff rates were 2 percent on raw materials such as silk, cotton, and wool; 11 percent on intermediate products such as silk, cotton yarn, and wool yarn; and 11 to 13 percent on final products such as fabrics, clothing, and carpets. Among the latter products, an average tariff rate of over 12 percent was levied on carpets and clothing. Reflecting Korea's advanced industrial structure and high wages, imports of textiles and apparel are rapidly increasing from China and other low-cost East Asian countries, while Korean exports in these sectors have been sluggish.

In addition to the statutory tariff rates mentioned above, adjustment tariffs have been imposed since 1993 on nine products (table 2.14). One example is HS 6302—toilet linen (a rate of 75 percent) and kitchen linen (a rate of 50 percent) made of cotton—where adjustment tariffs are used to protect the domestic industry from surging imports of lower-priced foreign products.

The relatively high tariffs mentioned above were reduced to less than 8 percent by 1994, and the application of adjustment tariffs to selected items was either terminated at the end of 1994 or reduced to lower rates.

Glass and Ceramic Products

In 1992, a tariff rate of 13 percent was imposed on imports of household glass products, imitation pearls, and some ceramic household products. Adjustment tariffs were also applied temporarily to articles made of mica and to refractory bricks (HS 6814 at a rate of 20 percent) during 1993 and to some cast and rolled glass (HS 7003 through 7005 at a rate of 40 percent) during 1993 and 1994.

Metal Products

Korea is ranked sixth in output volume among world iron and steel producers. By 1992, Korea no longer put special restrictions on the import of iron and steel. Furthermore, Korea maintains very low tariff rates on imports in this sector—2 to 5 percent on primary iron and steel and 10 to 11 percent on most forged and flat-rolled steel products. However, on some final iron and steel products, such as stoves, tables, and kitchen and other household articles, tariffs at the rate of 13 percent were imposed in 1992. The same rate was also applied to household articles made of aluminum. Adjustment tariffs of 20 percent were levied on iron and steel chains (HS 7315) and aluminum plates (HS 7606) during 1993 and 1994.

In 1994, all tariff rates on metal products were reduced to 2 to 5 percent on raw materials (such as pig iron and copper bars) and 8 percent on intermediate and finished products. Under the zero-for-zero tariff rate scheme, adopted in the Uruguay Round, Korea plans to abolish tariffs on a total of 47 HS four-digit items (including 35 iron and steel items and 6 nonferrous metals items) over the next 8 to 15 years. For 70 non-ferrous metal items not covered in the zero-for-zero scheme, Korea will cut its tariff rates by about half: that is, to about 4 percent. Tariff rates on metal products will therefore decline dramatically over the next decade.

Electronic Products

Since the 1980s, the Korean electronics industry has developed rapidly, constituting 13.5 percent of total production, 13.9 percent of total employment, and 27.0 percent of total exports in the overall manufacturing sector as of 1991. In 1993, exports of electronic products amounted to $22.2 billion, while imports were $12.3 billion (table 2.15). The electronics industry is expected to maintain a robust growth rate, both because income

Table 2.15   Importance of the electronics industry in Korea's external trade

	Year		
Economic indicator	1988	1990	1993
Exports (billions of dollars)	15.7	17.2	22.2
Imports (billions of dollars)	8.2	9.7	12.3
Exports as a share of output (percent)	66.8	59.0	61.7
Imports as a share of domestic demand (percent)	51.1	44.8	47.1

Source: Korean Ministry of Finance 1994.

elasticity of demand is high and because the "information era" will create new markets for electronic goods.

In 1992, a tariff of 13 percent was imposed on several electronics items, but most other tariffs were levied at rates of 10 to 11 percent. There were other forms of protection as well. Among the 258 (HS 10-digit) items on the list of products for import source diversification (i.e., to be purchased from sources other than Japan) in 1992, 50 items were electrical and electronic products (belonging to HS chapter 85). In addition, adjustment tariffs were levied in 1993 and 1994 on motherboards for computers (HS 8471, at rates of 24 and 20 percent; and HS 8473, at rates of 20 and 15 percent), on primary cells and batteries (HS 8506, at a rate of 30 percent), and on electrical resistors (HS 8533, at rates of 18 and 50 percent).

The tariff rates on electronics products were simplified to a uniform rate of 8 percent in 1994. This figure is a little higher than the average tariff imposed by the United States or Japan, but it is somewhat lower than the rates imposed by the European Union and Taiwan. Following the zero-for-zero tariff scheme and the general tariff reduction agreed in the Uruguay Round negotiations, Korea's tariff rates on electronic products will decline sharply over the next 10 years.

Transportation Equipment

The manufacture of transportation equipment, such as automobiles and ships, is a key export industry for the Korean economy. The Korean auto industry, in particular, has grown rapidly, both because of the spurt in Korea's income level and because of the surge in foreign demand for Korea's small cars (table 2.16). Until recently, Korea has imposed relatively high tariffs on automobile imports. Korea still imposes important nontariff barriers on automotive imports.

The tariff rates on miscellaneous automotive goods were between 11 and 13 percent in 1992, but the rates on motor vehicles for the transportation of persons (HS 8702 and HS 8703) and motor vehicles for the transpor-

Table 2.16 Production and trade in the automotive industry
(thousands of vehicles)

	1988	1990	1992	1993	1994	Average annual growth, 1988-94 (percent)
Total output	1,084.0	1,322.0	1,730.0	2,050.0	2,324.0	13.6
(passenger cars)	866.0	965.0	1,256.0	1,513.0	1,821.0	13.2
Exports	576.1	347.1	456.2	638.6	648.0	2.0
Imports	0.4	3.0	1.9	1.9	4.4	49.1

Sources: Korean Ministry of Trade and Industry; Korea Automotive Manufacturers' Association (KAMA) (quoted from Korean Ministry of Finance 1994).

tation of goods (HS 8704) were even higher—20 and 17 percent, respectively. All the tariff rates on vehicles were reduced to between 8 and 10 percent in 1994, and those on passenger cars were dropped to 8 percent.

In recent years, Korea's imports of automobiles rose rapidly from a very small base because of lower tariffs, rising demand in the domestic market, and aggressive US efforts to sell more American cars in Korea. However, Korean imports of many automotive products are still restricted under the "import source diversification system." In practice, this system amounts to a virtual ban on the import of small-sized and medium-sized passenger cars, and some trucks, from Japan. These vehicles require the recommendation and confirmation of the Korea Automotive Manufacturers' Association for importation. Such a recommendation was rarely given in the past, and this significant nontariff barrier contributed importantly to the development of Korea's strength in manufacturing small passenger cars.

The shipbuilding industry is another key exporting sector for Korea. During 1992, exports by Korea's shipbuilding industry equaled $41.1 billion, or about 90 percent of its production, and constituted 5.4 percent of Korea's total exports. No special import barriers existed in 1992. Tariff rates on most ships were zero or low (between 2.5 and 5 percent), although the rates on yachts and motorboats were higher (11 percent). On these, however, the rates were reduced to 8 percent in 1994.

Korean output of aircraft and parts is increasing rapidly, but this industry is still at an early stage of development. Imports supply 87 percent of total domestic demand. While the statutory tariff rates are 5 to 11 percent, special tariff abatements are allowed for aircraft components that are difficult to produce domestically (the abatement rates were 100 percent of the tariff in 1993 and 50 percent in 1994).

Miscellaneous Products

A tariff rate of 11 percent was applied to most musical instruments and other miscellaneous goods in 1992, and a higher rate of 13 percent was imposed on organs and electrical musical instruments (HS 9207), equipment for video games (HS 9504 and 9405), and sporting goods (HS 9506) in the same year. All these rates were simplified into the low uniform rate of 8 percent by 1994.

Highly Protected Sectors in 1992

This analysis focused on 49 sectors (106 items in the four-digit HS) that were highly protected in 1992. In selecting the products, two criteria were used:

- The collected tariff rate plus the tariff equivalent of other trade barriers must be no less than 12 percent.

- The import value should be no less than US$10 million (7.8 billion won), but exceptions are made for major items subject to prohibitive restraints (discussed below).[5]

Korea's most frequent tariff rate, the "central tariff rate" or modal rate, was 11 percent in 1992. With that knowledge, 12 percent was chosen as the threshold of high protection. Products such as milled rice (HS 1006), corn (HS 1005), pork (HS 0203), and soybeans (HS 1201), even with low tariff rates or with insignificant import volumes, are included in the list of highly protected products because severe nontariff barriers result in high differentials between domestic and world prices.

Table 2.17 illustrates the characteristics of the highly protected sectors in 1992 that are the focus of this volume.[6] The level of trade protection is measured for each product classified in the four-digit HS code, or for groups of products, on the basis of a "collected tariff rate" and the estimated tariff equivalent of total trade barriers. The collected tariff rate is defined as realized tariff revenues divided by the total import value (expressed on a c.i.f. basis). For agricultural products that were subject to quantitative restrictions as well as tariff barriers in 1992, "tariff equivalents" of quantitative restrictions are calculated from the differentials between domestic and world prices.

---

5. In principle, it would be better to express the size criterion in terms of domestic consumption. That approach was beyond the resources available; therefore an ad hoc effort was made to include imported products that are subject to prohibitive import barriers.

6. See also appendix table B.1 for base-year data on these sectors.

Table 2.17 Characteristics of highly protected sectors in South Korea

Sector and product (HS)	Collected tariff rate[a] (percent)	Nontariff barrier[b] (percent)	Tariff equivalent of tariff and NTB[c] (percent)	Production amount[d] (billion won)	Average growth rate (percent)	Import amount (billion won)	Average growth rate[e] (percent)	Ratio of production to imports
Agriculture and fish								
Beef (0202)	14.5	298.8	313.3	13,830.0	6.1	1,599.1	19.4	8.6
Pork (0203)	20.1	148.9	169.0	1,601.0	22.3	375.0	83.3	4.3
Poultry (0207)	20.8	30.2	51.0	1,251.0	4.5	2.0	9.6	625.5
Ivory, antlers, etc. (0507)	20.1	44.9	65.0	506.0	17.9	29.0	232.7	17.4
Dried onions and garlic (0712)	24.8	n.a.	n.a.	9.0	6.1	44.0	28.7	0.2
Dried beans (0713)	52.5	206.9	259.4	40.0	28.4	29.0	67.4	1.4
Nuts (0802)	30.0	463.8	493.8	60.0	(6.1)	11.9	34.2	5.0
Bananas (0803)	34.6	199.2	233.8	120.0	8.1	19.7	38.4	6.1
Peppers (0904)	85.0	n.a.	n.a.	3.0	(63.2)	63.2	76.8	0.0
Barley (1003)	38.9	261.1	300.0	1,041.0	14.7	11.0	13.8	94.6
—	34.9	389.5	424.4	293.0	(2.2)	9.7	32.0	30.2
Corn (1005)	2.6	362.4	365.0	24.0	(5.3)	664.5	10.0	0.0
Milled rice (1006)	5.0	590.0	595.0	6,723.0	2.9	0.4	6.0	16,807.5
Malt (1107)	35.1	263.9	299.0	115.0	14.0	17.3	157.2	6.6
Soybeans (1201)	3.0	538.0	541.0	199.0	(4.1)	259.2	3.1	0.8
Peanuts (1202)	40.3	215.8	256.1	51.0	(2.5)	8.8	44.3	5.8
Oilseeds (1207)	34.8	458.3	493.1	303.0	(5.6)	24.8	55.9	12.1
Fish (0301-2)	47.2	n.a.	n.a.	1,272.0	11.9	12.0	58.2	106.0
Crabs, lobster, and shrimp (0306)	17.7	n.a.	n.a.	219.0	14.3	17.6	0.0	12.4
Processed foods	29.1	12.9	42.0	8,887	12.2	476.0	42.6	18.7
Dairy products (0401-6)	21.5	128.6	150.1	1,861.0	13.0	26.5	23.0	70.2
Vegetable extracts (1302)	12.9	n.a.	n.a.	86.0	4.9	34.1	31.0	2.5
Prepared meat and fish (16)	25.3	n.a.	n.a.	2,179.0	7.5	30.7	55.8	71.0
Other sugars (1702)	17.6	n.a.	n.a.	184.0	2.4	10.2	19.0	18.0
Pasta (1902)	44.6	n.a.	n.a.	778.0	16.5	15.9	97.2	48.9
Prepared fruits and vegetables[c] (20)	43.1	n.a.	n.a.	641.0	27.3	167.7	50.7	3.8
Tea and roasted coffee (2101)	17.6	n.a.	n.a.	433.0	14.0	14.6	145.5	29.7
Sauces and prepared sauces (2103)	13.6	n.a.	n.a.	813.0	20.2	18.6	41.7	43.7
Other food preparations (2106)	13.1	n.a.	n.a.	739.0	16.9	65.7	62.8	11.2
Distilled liquor (2208)	39.5	n.a.	n.a.	847.0	4.6	38.5	33.8	22.0
Leaf tobacco (2401)	19.9	51.1	71.0	326.0	16.9	53.5	25.1	6.1

Product								
Chemical products	15.2	n.a.	n.a.	917.0	21.5	81.8	23.8	11.2
Natural steatite (2526)	12.4	n.a.	n.a.	23.0	9.7	12.1	17.4	1.9
Cosmetics (3304)	13.1	n.a.	n.a.	584.0	27.8	33.6	52.2	17.4
Toilet preparations (3307)	13.1	n.a.	n.a.	21.0	16.6	10.5	29.6	2.0
Casein (3501)	20.1	n.a.	n.a.	289.0	11.7	25.6	8.5	11.3
Textiles and light industries	14.7	n.a.	n.a.	9110.0	4.8	587.5	36.8	15.5
Plywood (4412)	15.0	n.a.	n.a.	509.0	3.5	274.5	35.3	1.9
Wooden tableware and kitchenware (4419)	46.6	n.a.	n.a.	22.0	(3.1)	8.0	53.0	2.8
Carpets (57)	13.0	n.a.	n.a.	59.0	11.3	21.6	10.4	2.7
Apparel (61, 62)	12.8	n.a.	n.a.	7,276.0	3.8	192.2	84.5	37.9
Other textile articles (63)	16.4	n.a.	n.a.	956.0	14.6	30.0	25.4	31.9
Porcelain household articles (6911)	13.1	n.a.	n.a.	188.0	9.9	11.8	18.1	15.9
Glassware (7013)	13.1	n.a.	n.a.	69.0	0.9	27.4	7.8	2.5
Glass beads and imitation pearls (7018)	13.0	n.a.	n.a.	31.0	15.4	22.0	15.8	1.4
Machinery and metal products	15.8	n.a.	n.a.	11,550.0	19.2	175.1	20.2	66.0
Stoves and ranges (7321)	13.1	n.a.	n.a.	385.0	33.9	20.7	4.1	18.6
Steel household articles (7323)	12.7	n.a.	n.a.	692.0	8.2	15.5	21.4	44.6
Aluminum household articles (7615)	13.0	n.a.	n.a.	132.0	7.2	8.7	39.1	15.2
Motor vehicles for people (8703)	16.3	n.a.	n.a.	7,735.0	18.0	45.3	0.4	170.8
Motor vehicles for goods (8704)	17.0	n.a.	n.a.	2,606.0	26.8	84.9	47.8	30.7
Miscellaneous goods	13.3	n.a.	n.a.	380.0	19.5	183.9	59.4	2.1
Electric musical instruments (9207)	12.5	n.a.	n.a.	113.0	67.9	9.5	15.4	11.9
Equipment for games (9504)	13.1	n.a.	n.a.	68.0	34.4	114.7	79.6	0.6
Sporting goods (9506)	13.7	n.a.	n.a.	199.0	7.1	59.7	48.5	3.3
Total for highly protected products	16.8	n.a.	n.a.	44,674.0	10.1	3103.4	25.5	14.4
All imports	6.3	n.a.	n.a.	244,416.0	13.8	63,771.0	12.1	3.8

a. Collected tariff rate is measured as tariff revenue divided by total import value, using the average annual exchange rate for 1992 ($1 = 780 won).
b. The nontariff barrier equals the tariff equivalent of the total difference between domest c and foreign prices, minus the tariff rate, where available. NTB estimates are only available for selected agricultural products; for all other products, t1e size of NTBs was not estimated in this study.
c. The tariff equivalents of the product categories comprising several subitems with different tariff equivalents are derived by taking the weighted average of individual products' tariff equivalents based on their production values for 1992.
d. Production values of individual products are calculated on the basis of the HSK-KSIC concordance in appendix table A8.
e. Average annual growth rates of production and imports are generally for the period of 1988–92.

Sources: Korea Customs Service 1993; Korean National Statistical Office 1994; Korean Ministry of Agriculture, Forestry, and Fisheries 1993; Economic Planning Board 1992; Uruguay Round Schedule LX 1994.

3

Estimation Results, Limitations, and Future Research

This chapter estimates the effects of trade protection on the 49 highly protected sectors in 1992 that are identified in chapter 2. The potential benefits of trade liberalization—which can also be viewed as the costs of trade protection—are measured by comparing two scenarios: a factual scenario, with actual economic magnitudes, and a counterfactual scenario, with potential values estimated assuming that protection is eliminated. The estimation model is explained in appendix A.

Ranges of calculated effects are presented in tables 3.2a and 3.2b. The estimates in table 3.2a are based on a "bundle" of five lower-end elasticity values (table 3.1a), while the estimates in table 3.2b are based on a "bundle" of five higher-end elasticity values (table 3.1b). Appendix B tabulates the effects of liberalization, sector by sector. The next several pages summarize the highlights.

Results of Estimation

Welfare Effect by Economic Agent

Welfare effects of removing protection can be summarized as follows: (1) consumer surplus gain, (2) producer surplus loss, (3) decline in the government's tariff revenue, together with elimination of import quota rents, and efficiency gain.

If all tariffs and quantitative restrictions were eliminated in Korea for the 49 products, the consumer surplus gain would have been about 9.2

Table 3.1a Group A: low parameter elasticity values used in partial computable equilibrium model

Sector and product (HS)	Edd	Edm	Emm	Emd	Es
Agriculture and fisheries					
Beef (0202)	0.20	0.14	0.71	0.50	0.20
Pork (0203)	0.20	0.14	9.43	6.60	0.20
Poultry (0207)	0.20	0.14	2.91	2.03	0.20
Ivory, antlers, etc. (0507)	1.22	0.85	0.20	0.14	0.20
Dried onions and garlic (0712)	0.22	0.16	0.20	0.14	0.20
Dried beans (0713)	0.20	0.14	0.77	0.54	0.20
Nuts (0802)	0.20	0.14	0.89	0.62	0.20
Bananas (0803)	3.00	2.10	0.20	0.14	0.20
Peppers (0904)	0.20	0.14	2.18	1.53	0.20
Barley (1003)	0.20	0.14	1.17	0.82	0.20
Corn (1005)	3.00	2.10	0.20	0.14	0.20
Milled rice (1006)	0.20	0.14	5.24	3.67	0.20
Malt (1107)	0.20	0.14	1.00	0.70	0.20
Soybeans (1201)	0.27	0.19	0.20	0.14	0.20
Peanuts (1202)	0.20	0.14	0.81	0.57	0.20
Oilseeds (1207)	0.20	0.14	0.67	0.47	0.20
Fish (0301-2)	0.20	0.14	4.61	3.23	0.20
Crabs, lobster, and shrimp (0306)	0.20	0.14	2.07	1.45	0.20
Processed foods					
Dairy products (0401-6)	0.30	0.21	2.91	2.04	0.30
Vegetable extracts (1302)	0.30	0.21	0.67	0.47	0.30
Prepared meat and fish (16)	0.30	0.21	5.75	4.03	0.30
Other sugars (1702)	0.30	0.21	4.50	3.15	0.30
Pasta (1902)	0.30	0.21	4.50	3.15	0.30
Prepared fruits and vegetables (20)	0.30	0.21	0.80	0.56	0.30
Tea and roasted coffee (2101)	0.30	0.21	4.50	3.15	0.30
Sauces and prepared sauces (2103)	0.30	0.21	4.50	3.15	0.30
Other food preparations (2106)	0.30	0.21	2.97	2.08	0.30
Distilled liquor (2208)	0.30	0.21	4.50	3.15	0.30
Leaf tobacco (2401)	0.30	0.21	1.54	1.08	0.30
Minerals and chemical products					
Natural steatite (2526)	0.40	0.28	0.68	0.48	0.40
Cosmetics (3304)	0.40	0.28	6.00	4.20	0.40
Toilet preparations (3307)	0.40	0.28	0.74	0.52	0.40
Casein (3501)	0.40	0.28	3.70	2.59	0.40
Textiles and light industries					
Plywood (4412)	0.50	0.35	0.81	0.56	0.50
Wooden tableware and kitchenware (4419)	0.50	0.35	0.94	0.66	0.50
Carpets (57)	0.50	0.35	1.19	0.83	0.50
Apparel (61, 62)	0.50	0.35	7.50	5.25	0.50
Other textile articles (63)	0.50	0.35	7.50	5.25	0.50
Porcelain household articles (6911)	0.50	0.35	6.93	4.85	0.50
Glassware (7013)	0.50	0.35	1.13	0.79	0.50
Glass beads and imitation pearls (7018)	0.50	0.35	0.62	0.44	0.50
Machinery and metal products					
Stoves and ranges (7321)	0.50	0.35	7.50	5.25	0.50
Steel household articles (7323)	0.50	0.35	7.50	5.25	0.50
Aluminum household articles (7615)	0.50	0.35	6.49	4.54	0.50
Motor vehicles for people (8703)	0.50	0.35	14.88	10.42	0.50
Motor vehicles for goods (8704)	0.50	0.35	7.50	5.25	0.50

Table 3.1a (continued)

Sector and product (HS)	Edd	Edm	Emm	Emd	Es
Miscellaneous goods					
Electric musical instruments (9207)	0.50	0.35	5.58	3.91	0.50
Equipment for games (9504)	0.96	0.67	0.50	0.35	0.50
Sporting goods (9506)	0.50	0.35	1.46	1.02	0.50

Edd = own-price elasticity of demand for the domestic commodity (the values are negative, but for ease of presentation, the minus sign is omitted).
Edm = cross-price elasticity of demand for the domestic commodity with respect to the price of the imported commodity.
Emm = own-price elasticity of demand for the imported commodity (the values are negative, but for ease of presentation, the minus sign is omitted).
Emd = cross-price elasticity of demand for the imported commodity with respect to the price of the domestic commodity.
Es = own-price elasticity of supply for the domestic good.

trillion to 10.4 trillion won in 1992 (about 3.8 to 4.3 percent of GNP), the producer surplus loss would have amounted to 6.5 trillion to 7.0 trillion won (2.7 to 2.9 percent of GNP), the government's tariff revenue would have declined by 0.4 trillion won (12.8 percent of the government's total tariff revenues), import quota rents of 1.0 trillion won would have been eliminated, and the efficiency gain would have amounted to 0.8 trillion to 2.5 trillion won (0.3 to 1.0 percent of GNP). Reversing the signs, these effects can be read as the costs of protection to Korea (tables 3.2a and 3.2b).

Consumer Surplus

With a decline in the prices of imported and domestic goods due to the removal of protection, the consumer surplus gain would amount to an estimated 9.2 trillion to 10.4 trillion won in 1992.[1] This figure would represent 19 to 22 percent of domestic sales (domestic production plus imports) accounted for by the 49 sectors (domestic sales were 47.8 trillion won); it would also amount to 3.0 to 3.4 percent of the total domestic market for tradeable goods (agricultural, mining, and manufacturing products), for which sales amounted to 308 trillion won in 1992.

The consumer gain from agricultural and fishery products is estimated to be 6.6 trillion to 7.5 trillion won, which explains about 73 percent of the total calculated gains in consumer surplus. The big items are milled rice (3.5 trillion to 3.7 trillion won, or 35 to 38 percent of total consumer gains), beef (771 billion to 993 billion won), corn (583 billion to 668 billion won), peppers (426 billion to 450 billion won), and soybeans (350 billion to 411 billion won). The consumer surplus gains would be 1.4 trillion to

---

1. The word "consumer" encompasses firms that purchase goods as intermediate inputs, as well as households that purchase final consumption goods. However, because almost all of the highly protected products listed in table 2.17 are final consumption goods, most of them are purchased by private households.

Table 3.1b Group B: high parameter elasticity values used in partial computable equilibrium model

Sector and product (HS)	Edd	Edm	Emm	Emm	Es
Agriculture and fisheries					
Beef (0202)	0.50	0.35	1.78	1.25	0.50
Pork (0203)	0.50	0.35	12.20	8.54	0.50
Poultry (0207)	0.50	0.35	7.27	5.09	0.50
Ivory, antlers, etc. (0507)	3.05	2.14	0.50	0.35	0.50
Dried onions and garlic (0712)	0.56	0.39	0.50	0.35	0.50
Dried beans (0713)	0.50	0.35	1.93	1.35	0.50
Nuts (0802)	0.50	0.35	2.23	1.56	0.50
Bananas (0803)	7.50	5.25	0.50	0.35	0.50
Peppers (0904)	0.50	0.35	2.93	2.05	0.50
Barley (1003)	0.50	0.35	1.73	1.21	0.50
Corn (1005)	7.50	5.25	0.50	0.35	0.50
Milled rice (1006)	0.50	0.35	5.80	4.06	0.50
Malt (1107)	0.50	0.35	2.51	1.76	0.50
Soybeans (1201)	0.67	0.47	0.50	0.35	0.50
Peanuts (1202)	0.50	0.35	2.02	1.41	0.50
Oilseeds (1207)	0.50	0.35	1.09	0.76	0.50
Fish (0301-2)	0.50	0.35	7.10	4.97	0.50
Crabs, lobster, and shrimp (0306)	0.50	0.35	5.17	3.62	0.50
Processed foods					
Dairy products (0401-6)	0.75	0.53	4.01	2.81	0.75
Vegetable extracts (1302)	0.75	0.53	1.68	1.18	0.75
Prepared meat and fish (16)	0.75	0.53	11.25	7.88	0.75
Other sugars (1702)	0.75	0.53	11.25	7.88	0.75
Pasta (1902)	0.75	0.53	11.25	7.88	0.75
Prepared fruits and vegetables (20)	0.75	0.53	2.00	1.40	0.75
Tea and roasted coffee (2101)	0.75	0.53	11.25	7.88	0.75
Sauces and prepared sauces (2103)	0.75	0.53	11.25	7.88	0.75
Other food preparations (2106)	0.75	0.53	7.43	5.20	0.75
Distilled liquor (2208)	0.75	0.53	11.25	7.88	0.75
Leaf tobacco (2401)	0.75	0.53	3.85	2.70	0.75
Minerals and chemical products					
Natural steatite (2526)	1.00	0.70	1.71	1.19	1.00
Cosmetics (3304)	1.00	0.70	15.00	10.50	1.00
Toilet preparations (3307)	1.00	0.70	1.86	1.30	1.00
Casein (3501)	1.00	0.70	9.26	6.48	1.00
Textiles and light industries					
Plywood (4412)	1.50	1.05	2.42	1.69	1.50
Wooden tableware and kitchenware (4419)	1.50	1.05	2.81	1.97	1.50
Carpets (57)	1.50	1.05	3.56	2.49	1.50
Apparel (61, 62)	1.50	1.05	22.50	15.75	1.50
Other textile articles (63)	1.50	1.05	22.50	15.75	1.50
Porcelain household articles (6911)	1.50	1.05	20.78	14.55	1.50
Glassware (7013)	1.50	1.05	3.39	2.37	1.50
Glass beads and imitation pearls (7018)	1.50	1.05	1.87	1.31	1.50
Machinery and metal products					
Stoves and ranges (7321)	1.25	0.88	18.75	13.13	1.25
Steel household articles (7323)	1.25	0.88	18.75	13.13	1.25
Aluminum household articles (7615)	1.25	0.88	16.23	11.36	1.25
Motor vehicles for people (8703)	1.25	0.88	21.74	15.22	1.25
Motor vehicles for goods (8704)	1.25	0.88	18.75	13.13	1.25

Table 3.1b (continued)

Sector and product (HS)	Edd	Edm	Emm	Emm	Es
Miscellaneous goods					
Electric musical instruments (9207)	2.00	1.40	22.32	15.62	2.00
Equipment for games (9504)	3.84	2.69	2.00	1.40	2.00
Sporting goods (9506)	2.00	1.40	5.84	4.09	2.00

Edd = own-price elasticity of demand for the domestic commodity (the values are negative, but for ease of presentation, the minus sign is omitted).
Edm = cross-price elasticity of demand for the domestic commodity with respect to the price of the imported commodity.
Emm = own-price elasticity of demand for the imported commodity (the values are negative, but for ease of presentation, the minus sign is omitted).
Emd = cross-price elasticity of demand for the imported commodity with respect to the price of the domestic commodity.
Es = own-price elasticity of supply for the domestic good.

1.8 trillion won in processed foods, concentrated largely in dairy products (555 billion to 592 billion won). Machinery and metal products would exhibit gains of 630 billion to 690 billion won. But the effect in the textiles and light industries sector would be relatively insignificant. Consumer gains in passenger cars (413 billion to 426 billion won) and apparel (344 billion to 411 billion won) would be the largest among manufactured goods.

Producer Surplus

Because of lower prices for domestic goods, and also because of the larger import volumes after liberalization, domestic producers would lose about 6.5 trillion to 7.0 trillion won in 1992. This figure would represent 14 to 15 percent of domestic output from these sectors and 2.1 to 2.3 percent of total domestic output in the agriculture, fisheries, and manufacturing sectors in 1992. Producer losses would be greatest on milled rice, at an estimated 2.8 trillion to 3.1 trillion won, or about 44 percent of total producer losses.

Tariff Revenue and Quota Rents

The decrease in the government's tariff revenue from removing protection would amount to an estimated 409 billion won in 1992. The quota rents accruing to quota holders and importers, which would disappear following the removal of nontariff barriers, equal 984 billion won, all from the agriculture, fisheries, and dairy products sectors. Quota rents are largely captured by domestic economic agents, as explained below.

Efficiency

Trade liberalization would bring efficiency gains by correcting distortions in the price system. Efficiency gains measure net gains in national welfare,

Table 3.2a Group A: estimated static welfare effects of removing protection, 1992
(billions of won, except where noted)

Sector and product (HS)	Consumer surplus gain[a] (A+B+C+D)	Producer surplus loss (A)	Tariff revenue decline (B)	Quota rents eliminated[b] (C)	Efficiency gain (D)	Consumer surplus ratio[c] (percent)	Production plus imports
Agriculture and fisheries	6,649	4,861	175	960	653	43.1	15,430.0
Beef (0202)	771	453	63	173	82	39.0	1,976.0
Pork (0203)	172	166	0	1	6	13.7	1,253.0
Poultry (0207)	103	80	5	7	11	19.3	535.0
Ivory, antlers, etc. (0507)	10	1	9	n.a.	0	18.9	53.0
Dried onions and garlic (0712)	37	14	10	11	2	53.6	69.0
Dried beans (0713)	45	26	3	7	9	62.5	72.0
Nuts (0802)	63	40	5	9	9	44.3	140.0
Bananas (0803)	31	1	29	n.a.	1	47.0	66.0
Peppers (0904)	426	382	3	5	36	40.5	1,052.0
Barley (1003)	143	122	3	5	13	47.2	303.0
Corn (1005)	583	14	17	505	47	84.6	689.0
Milled rice (1006)	3,469	3,102	0	0	367	51.6	6,723.0
Malt (1107)	66	42	4	8	12	50.8	132.0
Soybeans (1201)	350	97	8	211	34	76.4	458.0
Peanuts (1202)	29	18	3	4	4	46.7	60.0
Oilseeds (1207)	167	132	6	14	15	51.2	328.0
Fish (0301-2)	168	159	4	0	5	13.1	1,284.0
Crabs, lobster, and shrimp (0306)	15	12	3	0	0	6.3	237.0
Processed foods	1,289	1,066	105	24	94	13.8	9,365.0
Dairy products (0401-6)	555	487	5	11	52	29.4	1,887.0
Vegetable extracts (1302)	8	4	4	0	0	6.7	120.0
Prepared meat and fish (16)	174	163	6	0	5	7.9	2,210.0
Other sugars (1702)	13	10	2	0	1	6.2	194.0
Pasta (1902)	103	92	5	0	6	13.0	794.0
Prepared fruits and vegetables (20)	131	74	51	0	6	16.2	809.0
Tea and roasted coffee (2101)	27	24	2	0	1	6.0	448.0
Sauces and prepared sauces (2103)	38	35	2	0	1	4.6	832.0

Product							
Other food preparations (2106)	40	31	8	0	1	5.0	805.0
Distilled liquor (2208)	114	92	11	0	11	12.9	886.0
Leaf tobacco (2401)	86	54	9	13	10	22.7	379.0
Minerals and chemical products	56	44	10	0	2	5.7	999.0
Natural steatite (2526)	2	1	1	0	0	5.7	35.0
Cosmetics (3304)	29	24	4	0	1	4.9	618.0
Toilet preparations (3307)	2	1	1	0	0	6.5	31.0
Casein (3501)	23	18	4	0	1	7.3	315.0
Textiles and light industries	493	400	75	0	18	5.1	9,699.0
Plywood (4412)	62	24	36	0	2	7.8	784.0
Wooden tableware and kitchenware (4419)	6	3	3	0	0	20.0	30.0
Carpets (57)	4	2	2	0	0	6.2	81.0
Apparel (61, 62)	345	310	23	0	12	4.6	7,468.0
Other textile articles (63)	56	49	4	0	3	5.7	986.0
Porcelain household articles (6911)	10	8	1	0	1	5.0	200.0
Glassware (7013)	6	3	3	0	0	6.3	96.0
Glass beads and imitation pearls (7018)	4	1	3	0	0	7.5	53.0
Machinery and metal products	627	579	23	0	25	5.4	11,725.0
Stoves and ranges (7321)	19	16	2	0	1	4.9	406.0
Steel household articles (7323)	31	28	2	0	1	4.2	707.0
Aluminum household articles (7615)	6	5	1	0	0	5.0	141.0
Motor vehicles for people (8703)	413	393	6	0	14	5.3	7,780.0
Motor vehicles for goods (8704)	158	137	12	0	9	5.9	2,691.0
Miscellaneous goods	40	18	21	0	1	6.9	565.0
Electric musical instruments (9207)	6	5	1	0	0	4.9	122.0
Equipment for games (9504)	17	4	13	0	0	9.3	183.0
Sporting goods (9506)	17	9	7	0	1	6.2	259.0
Total for highly protected products	9,154	6,968	409	984	793	19.2	47,783.0

n.a. = not available

a. Consumer surplus gain includes gains on both domestic and imported goods.

b. Quota rents eliminated refers to the decrease in import price by removing nontariff barriers and is additional to the decline in tariff revenue.

c. The consumer surplus ratio is defined as the consumer surplus gain divided by the sum of domestic production and imports before liberalization.

Table 3.2b Group B: estimated static welfare effects of removing protection, 1992
(billions of won, except where noted)

Sector and product (HS)	Consumer surplus gain[a] (A+B+C+D)	Producer surplus loss (A)	Tariff revenue decline (B)	Quota rents eliminated[b] (C)	Efficiency gain (D)	Consumer surplus ratio[c] (percent)	Production plus imports
Agriculture and fisheries	7,503	4,499	175	960	1,869	48.7	15,430.0
Beef (0202)	993	431	63	173	326	50.3	1,976.0
Pork (0203)	178	162	0	1	15	14.2	1,253.0
Poultry (0207)	173	78	5	7	83	32.3	535.0
Ivory, antlers, etc. (0507)	10	1	9	n.a.	0	18.9	53.0
Dried onions and garlic (0712)	37	14	10	11	2	53.6	69.0
Dried beans (0713)	95	24	3	7	61	131.9	72.0
Nuts (0802)	96	37	5	9	45	68.6	140.0
Bananas (0803)	33	1	29	n.a.	3	50.0	66.0
Peppers (0904)	449	357	3	5	84	42.8	1,052.0
Barley (1003)	151	113	3	5	30	49.8	303.0
Corn (1005)	668	12	17	505	134	97.0	689.0
Milled rice (1006)	3,669	2,836	0	0	833	54.6	6,723.0
Malt (1107)	133	39	4	8	82	102.3	132.0
Soybeans (1201)	411	88	8	211	104	89.7	458.0
Peanuts (1202)	42	16	3	4	19	70.0	60.0
Oilseeds (1207)	176	122	6	14	34	54.0	328.0
Fish (0301-2)	173	156	4	0	13	13.5	1,284.0
Crabs, lobster, and shrimp (0306)	16	12	3	0	1	6.8	237.0
Processed foods	1,502	1,023	105	24	350	16.0	9,364.0
Dairy products (0401-6)	592	456	5	11	120	31.4	1,887.0
Vegetable extracts (1302)	8	4	4	0	0	6.7	120.0
Prepared meat and fish (16)	185	161	6	0	18	8.4	2,210.0
Other sugars (1702)	14	10	2	0	2	7.2	194.0
Pasta (1902)	149	90	5	0	54	18.8	794.0
Prepared fruits and vegetables (20)	141	72	51	0	18	17.4	809.0
Tea and roasted coffee (2101)	28	23	2	0	3	6.5	448.0
Sauces and prepared sauces (2103)	39	35	2	0	2	4.7	832.0

Other food preparations (2106)	43	31	8	0	4	5.2	805.0
Distilled liquor (2208)	187	89	11	0	87	21.1	886.0
Leaf tobacco (2401)	116	52	9	13	42	30.6	379.0
Minerals and chemical products	65	43	10	0	12	6.5	999.0
Natural steatite (2526)	2	1	1	0	0	5.7	35.0
Cosmetics (3304)	34	24	4	0	6	5.5	618.0
Toilet preparations (3307)	2	1	1	0	0	6.5	31.0
Casein (3501)	27	17	4	0	6	8.6	315.0
Textiles and light industries	590	391	75	0	124	6.1	9,699.0
Plywood (4412)	64	23	36	0	5	8.2	784.0
Wooden tableware and kitchenware (4419)	8	3	3	0	2	23.3	30.0
Carpets (57)	5	2	2	0	1	6.2	81.0
Apparel (61, 62)	411	303	23	0	85	5.5	7,468.0
Other textile articles (63)	78	48	4	0	26	7.9	986.0
Porcelain household articles (6911)	13	8	1	0	4	6.5	200.0
Glassware (7013)	7	3	3	0	1	7.3	96.0
Glass beads and imitation pearls (7018)	4	1	3	0	0	7.5	53.0
Machinery and metal products	690	569	23	0	98	5.9	11,725.0
Stoves and ranges (7321)	24	16	2	0	6	5.9	406.0
Steel household articles (7323)	34	28	2	0	4	4.7	707.0
Aluminum household articles (7615)	8	5	1	0	2	6.4	141.0
Motor vehicles for people (8703)	426	385	6	0	35	5.5	7,780.0
Motor vehicles for goods (8704)	198	135	12	0	51	7.4	2,691.0
Miscellaneous goods	44	16	21	0	7	8.0	565.0
Electric musical instruments (9207)	8	4	1	0	3	7.4	122.0
Equipment for games (9504)	18	4	13	0	1	9.8	183.0
Sporting goods (9506)	18	8	7	0	3	6.9	259.0
Total for highly protected products	10,394	6,541	409	984	2,460	21.8	47,783.0

n.a. = not available

a. Consumer surplus gain includes gains on both domestic and imported goods.

b. Quota rents eliminated refers to the decrease in import price by removing nontariff barriers and is additional to the decline in tariff revenue.

c. The consumer surplus ratio is defined as the consumer surplus gain divided by the sum of domestic production and imports before liberalization.

taking into account gains in consumer surplus, losses in producer surplus, the decline in tariff revenue, and the drop in quota rents accruing to domestic economic agents. Efficiency gains would amount to 0.8 trillion to 2.5 trillion won. Some 76 to 82 percent of the effect would be accounted for in the agriculture and fisheries sectors (0.7 trillion to 1.9 trillion won).

The effect of eliminating quotas and other quantitative restrictions would essentially amount to a transfer to domestic consumers from domestic producers. In Korea, quota rents from nontariff barriers on highly protected products are largely captured by the government or by public institutions (e.g., the Livestock Product Marketing Corporation) that control import licenses.[2] These quota rents are largely used to pay subsidies to domestic producers of the same goods. With lower domestic prices, domestic consumers would benefit, but domestic producers would receive lower subsidies.

Effects on Domestic Production and Imports

Trade liberalization in the 49 highly protected products would cause imports to rise by 2.9 trillion to 10.9 trillion won (3.7 billion to 14.0 billion dollars). This represents an import surge of 94 to 350 percent of the actual import of the 49 products in 1992. In particular, agriculture and fisheries imports are calculated to increase by 1.7 trillion to 5.1 trillion won (accounting for 47 to 56 percent of the total import gains). Moreover, if we add the increase of 0.5 trillion to 2.0 trillion won in processed foods, which are closely related to the agriculture and fisheries sector, some 66 to 75 percent of the total import gains are accounted for by agriculture-related imports. Machinery and metal products (0.4 trillion to 1.4 trillion won) and textiles and light industries products (0.3 trillion to 2.0 trillion won) each contribute about 13 percent of the total increase in imports. The estimated increase in imports of chemical products and miscellaneous goods is very small.

In examining the rise in imports by item, sharp increases are expected in milled rice (857 billion to 1,945 billion won), dairy products (172 billion to 399 billion won), peppers (97 billion to 225 billion won), corn (120 trillion to 342 trillion won), beef (262 billion to 1,037 billion won), and distilled liquor (81 billion to 612 billion won), all of which have high tariff equivalents. Big increases are also expected in passenger cars (202 billion to 495 billion won), trucks (122 billion to 699 billion won), and apparel (200 billion to 1,435 billion won), where current import volumes are relatively small compared with the size of the domestic market (tables 3.3a and 3.3b).

---

2. By contrast, in some other countries, quota rents are mainly captured by foreign firms and represent a net cost to the economy, rather than a shuffling of benefits between consumers and producers.

Table 3.3a Group A: estimated impact of removing protection on imports and production

Sector and product (HS)	Increase in imports (billion won)	Increase in imports (percent)	Decrease in production (billion won)	Decrease in production (percent)
Agriculture and fishery	1,716	107	1,281	9
Beef (0202)	262	70	107	7
Pork (0203)	36	1,780	36	3
Poultry (0207)	58	200	17	3
Ivory, antlers, etc. (0507)	1	3	0	3
Dried onions and garlic (0712)	6	21	4	9
Dried beans (0713)	22	182	7	12
Nuts (0802)	25	125	10	8
Bananas (0803)	4	7	0	8
Peppers (0904)	97	879	96	9
Barley (1003)	32	327	32	11
Corn (1005)	120	18	4	18
Milled rice (1006)	857	214,219	853	13
Malt (1107)	32	185	11	9
Soybeans (1201)	79	31	28	14
Peanuts (1202)	10	117	4	9
Oilseeds (1207)	36	146	36	12
Fish (0301-2)	34	284	34	3
Crabs, lobster, and shrimp (0306)	5	29	2	1
Processed foods	482	101	354	4
Dairy products (0401-6)	172	649	171	9
Vegetable extracts (1302)	2	6	1	1
Prepared meat and fish (16)	51	166	51	2
Other sugars (1702)	7	73	3	2
Pasta (1902)	40	250	30	4
Prepared fruits and vegetables (20)	41	24	24	4
Tea and roasted coffee (2101)	11	73	7	2
Sauces and prepared sauces (2103)	10	54	11	1
Other food preparations (2106)	21	32	9	1
Distilled liquor (2208)	81	210	29	3
Leaf tobacco (2401)	46	87	18	5
Minerals and chemical products	44	54	17	2
Natural steatite (2526)	1	6	0	2
Cosmetics (3304)	25	75	10	2
Toilet preparations (3307)	1	7	0	2
Casein (3501)	17	67	7	3
Textiles and light industries	285	48	203	2
Plywood (4412)	24	9	12	2
Wooden tableware and kitchenware (4419)	2	31	1	6
Carpets (57)	3	12	1	2
Apparel (61, 62)	200	104	158	2
Other textile articles (63)	41	136	25	3
Porcelain household articles (6911)	11	90	4	2
Glassware (7013)	3	11	1	2
Glass beads and imitation pearls (7018)	1	6	1	2

(continued)

Table 3.3a (continued)

Sector and product (HS)	Increase in imports		Decrease in production	
	(billion won)	(percent)	(billion won)	(percent)
Machinery and metal products	367	210	298	3
Stoves and ranges (7321)	21	101	8	2
Steel household articles (7323)	15	97	14	2
Aluminum household articles (7615)	7	82	3	2
Motor vehicles for people (8703)	202	445	202	3
Motor vehicles for goods (8704)	122	143	71	3
Miscellaneous goods	20	11	8	2
Electric musical instruments (9207)	6	64	2	2
Equipment for games (9504)	5	4	2	3
Sporting goods (9506)	9	15	4	2
Total for highly protected products	2,914	94	2,161	5

Although increased imports, resulting from trade liberalization, might exert an adverse effect on the trade balance in the short run. This impact on the trade balance is likely to be smaller than the change in imports. Trade liberalization prompts some labor and capital to move from protected sectors to other parts of the economy. In the process, it improves the productivity of the economy and enhances exports in sectors with a competitive edge. These long-run effects might actually improve the trade balance.

The decline in the price of imported goods and the accompanying increase in import volumes after trade liberalization would cause domestic production in the affected sectors to decline. The decline in domestic output for the 49 items is estimated at about 2.2 trillion to 5.2 trillion won, which accounts for 5 to 12 percent of actual production of these items in 1992.

The agricultural and fisheries sector, which operates with a high level of protection, would be affected the most. The decline of 1.3 trillion to 2.9 trillion won in this sector would account for more than half of the total production decline of all 49 sectors. Other hard-hit sectors would be processed foods (354 billion to 846 billion won, or about 16 percent of the total production decline), machinery and metal products (298 billion to 729 billion won, or about 14 percent of the total production decline), and textile and other light industries (203 billion to 600 billion won, or 9 to 12 percent of the total production decline).

As for individual items, the production decline in milled rice would reach 0.9 trillion to 1.9 trillion won, about 38 percent of the total decline in production of all highly protected items. In addition, there would be sharp declines in the production of beef (107 billion to 255 billion won), dairy products (171 billion to 398 billion won), and peppers (96 billion to 224 billion won). Among manufactured goods, passenger cars (202

Table 3.3b Group B: estimated impact of removing protection on imports and production

Sector and product (HS)	Increase in imports (billion won)	Increase in imports (percent)	Decrease in production (billion won)	Decrease in production (percent)
Agriculture and fisheries	5,143	322	2,942	21
Beef (0202)	1,037	277	255	16
Pork (0203)	87	4,352	87	7
Poultry (0207)	423	1,459	42	8
Ivory, antlers, etc. (0507)	3	7	1	6
Dried onions and garlic (0712)	18	61	8	21
Dried beans (0713)	147	1,232	16	27
Nuts (0802)	130	658	23	19
Bananas (0803)	11	18	1	18
Peppers (0904)	225	2,047	224	22
Barley (1003)	75	771	74	25
Corn (1005)	342	52	10	40
Milled rice (1006)	1,945	486,365	1,934	29
Malt (1107)	220	1,270	25	22
Soybeans (1201)	246	95	62	31
Peanuts (1202)	52	594	10	20
Oilseeds (1207)	83	333	81	27
Fish (0301-2)	83	694	83	7
Crabs, lobster, and shrimp (0306)	16	89	6	3
Processed foods	2,040	428	846	10
Dairy products (0401-6)	399	1,504	398	21
Vegetable extracts (1302)	6	17	3	3
Prepared meat and fish (16)	178	579	125	6
Other sugars (1702)	30	296	8	4
Pasta (1902)	349	2,193	72	9
Prepared fruits and vegetables (20)	121	72	58	9
Tea and roasted coffee (2101)	43	296	18	4
Sauces and prepared sauces (2103)	36	195	27	3
Other food preparations (2106)	65	99	23	3
Distilled liquor (2208)	612	1,590	71	8
Leaf tobacco (2401)	201	375	43	13
Minerals and chemical products	173	211	45	5
Natural steatite (2526)	2	16	1	4
Cosmetics (3304)	102	303	25	4
Toilet preparations (3307)	2	19	1	4
Casein (3501)	67	260	18	6
Textiles and light industries	1,983	337	600	7
Plywood (4412)	80	29	36	7
Wooden tableware and kitchenware (4419)	10	125	4	18
Carpets (57)	8	39	4	6
Apparel (61, 62)	1,435	747	465	6
Other textile articles (63)	366	1,219	73	8
Porcelain household articles (6911)	70	590	12	6
Glassware (7013)	10	37	4	6
Glass beads and imitation pearls (7018)	4	19	2	6

(continued)

Table 3.3b (continued)

Sector and product (HS)	Increase in imports (billion won)	Increase in imports (percent)	Decrease in production (billion won)	Decrease in production (percent)
Machinery and metal products	1,391	795	729	6
Stoves and ranges (7321)	98	471	20	5
Steel household articles (7323)	69	443	35	5
Aluminum household articles (7615)	30	347	7	5
Motor vehicles for people (8703)	495	1,092	494	6
Motor vehicles for goods (8704)	699	823	173	7
Miscellaneous goods	126	68	33	9
Electric musical instruments (9207)	60	628	9	8
Equipment for games (9504)	21	18	7	11
Sporting goods (9506)	45	76	17	9
Total for highly protected products	10,856	350	5,195	12

billion to 494 billion won), apparel (158 billion to 465 billion won), and trucks (71 billion to 173 billion won) would experience the sharpest declines in production.

Effects on Employment

The decline in domestic production of the sectors would cause a drop in domestic employment in these sectors as well. Assuming that employment changes proportionally to changes in production, the number of jobs would decline by 174,000 to 405,000 workers, or 8 to 19 percent of total employment in the 49 sectors (tables 3.4a and 3.4b).

The decrease in agriculture and fisheries jobs would reach 162,000 to 372,000 workers, over 90 percent of the total decrease in the 49 sectors. Other sectors worth mentioning are textile and light industries (6,000 to 18,000 workers), processed foods (4,000 to 9,000 workers), and machinery and metal products (2,000 to 5,000 workers).

Because most Korean farmers raise several kinds of crops and animals at the same time, the employment numbers for individual items in tables 3.4a and 3.4b represent full-time equivalent jobs for many part-time slices of the agrarian work force. The employment number for each product is calculated by multiplying the total number of agricultural employees by the share of each product in total agricultural production. According to this method, employment in milled rice is estimated to decline by 110,000 to 250,000 workers, which would account for about 62 percent of the total decline in employment.

In the case of manufacturing goods, only the decline in employment in the apparel sector (5,000 to 14,000 workers) is relatively large.

By combining figures on the adverse employment effects of trade liberalization with the positive effects on consumer surplus or economic effi-

Table 3.4a Group A: estimated employment effects of removing protection

Sector and product (HS)	Employment before liberalization[a] (thousands of workers)	Loss of employment (thousands of workers)	(percent)	Cost of preserving a job Consumer cost (million won)	Efficiency cost (million won)
Agriculture and fisheries	1,651.9	162.41	9.8	40.9	4.0
Beef (0202)	207.1	13.93	6.7	56.0	6.0
Pork (0203)	161.8	4.60	2.8	37.0	1.0
Poultry (0207)	65.4	2.25	3.4	46.0	5.0
Ivory, antlers, etc. (0507)	1.2	0.03	2.5	316.0	2.0
Dried onions and garlic (0712)	5.2	0.47	9.0	80.0	5.0
Dried beans (0713)	7.8	0.91	11.7	49.0	10.0
Nuts (0802)	14.5	1.17	8.1	53.0	7.0
Bananas (0803)	0.4	0.03	7.5	992.0	32.0
Peppers (0904)	134.7	12.46	9.3	34.0	3.0
Barley (1003)	37.9	4.15	10.9	34.0	3.0
Corn (1005)	3.1	0.57	18.4	1,029.0	83.0
Milled rice (1006)	869.6	110.36	12.7	31.0	3.0
Malt (1107)	14.9	1.38	9.3	49.0	9.0
Soybeans (1201)	25.8	3.57	13.8	98.0	9.0
Peanuts (1202)	6.6	0.56	8.5	49.0	7.0
Oilseeds (1207)	39.2	4.59	11.7	37.0	3.0
Fish (0301-2)	48.4	1.29	2.7	130.0	4.0
Crabs, lobster, and shrimp (0306)	8.3	0.09	1.1	160.0	4.0
Processed foods	115.9	3.53	3.0	365.2	26.6
Dairy products (0401-6)	11.5	1.06	9.2	526.0	49.0
Vegetable extracts (1302)	1.1	0.00	1.1	598.0	9.8
Prepared meat and fish (16)	39.8	0.93	2.3	188.0	6.0
Other sugars (1702)	1.5	0.03	2.0	480.0	22.0
Pasta (1902)	10.8	0.41	3.8	252.0	15.0
Prepared fruits and vegetables (20)	11.4	0.42	3.7	311.0	15.0
Tea and roasted coffee (2101)	2.5	0.04	1.6	632.0	19.0
Sauces and prepared sauces (2103)	7.6	0.10	1.3	377.0	6.0
Other food preparations (2106)	23.7	0.30	1.3	131.0	4.0
Distilled liquor (2208)	4.3	0.15	3.5	771.0	77.0
Leaf tobacco (2401)	1.7	0.09	5.3	925.0	103.0
Minerals and chemical products	9.6	0.19	2.0	300.0	10.5
Natural steatite (2526)	0.4	0.01	2.5	353.0	6.0
Cosmetics (3304)	5.8	0.10	1.7	300.0	15.0
Toilet preparations (3307)	0.2	0.00	0.2	626.0	13.0
Casein (3501)	3.2	0.08	3.0	289.0	18.0

(continued)

Table 3.4a (continued)

Sector and product (HS)	Employment before liberalization[a] (thousands of workers)	Loss of employment (thousands of workers)	(percent)	Cost of preserving a job Consumer cost (million won)	Efficiency cost (million won)
Textiles and light industries	269.9	6.05	2.2	81.3	3.0
Plywood (4412)	6.7	0.16	2.4	379.0	10.0
Wooden tableware and kitchenware (4419)	1.2	0.08	6.7	72.0	5.0
Carpets (57)	1.3	0.03	2.3	184.0	5.0
Apparel (61, 62)	225.4	4.91	2.2	70.0	2.0
Other textile articles (63)	23.7	0.62	2.6	90.0	5.0
Porcelain household articles (6911)	9.2	0.20	2.2	50.0	3.0
Glassware (7013)	2.1	0.04	1.9	139.0	4.0
Glass beads and imitation pearls (7018)	0.3	0.01	3.3	613.0	12.0
Machinery and metal products	86.7	2.16	2.5	291.7	11.6
Stoves and ranges (7321)	3.9	0.08	2.1	237.0	15.0
Steel household articles (7323)	17.2	0.36	2.1	86.0	2.0
Aluminum household articles (7615)	3.2	0.07	2.2	102.0	6.0
Motor vehicles for people (8703)	46.7	1.22	2.6	339.0	12.0
Motor vehicles for goods (8704)	15.7	0.43	2.7	373.0	21.0
Miscellaneous goods	6.6	0.15	2.3	260.0	6.7
Electric musical instruments (9207)	0.6	0.01	1.7	483.0	28.0
Equipment for games (9504)	1.0	0.03	3.0	619.0	10.0
Sporting goods (9506)	5.0	0.11	2.2	148.0	5.0
Total for highly protected products	2,140.6	174.49	8.2	52.5	4.5

a. In agriculture, employment for individual commodities is calculated as the number of total agricultural employees multiplied by the production weight for each commodity. Because most Korean farmers raise several different crops and livestock concurrently, employment for individual commodities does not correspond to identifiable farmers raising just that item.

Sources: Korean National Statistical Office, 1994; Korean Ministry of Agriculture, Forestry, and Fisheries, 1993.

ciency, the welfare cost of preserving a job through trade protection can be calculated. By this arithmetic, the estimated cost of saving a job through trade protection is 26 million to 53 million won ($33,000 to $67,000) in consumer surplus loss and 5 million to 6 million won ($6,000 to $8,000) in efficiency loss.

In terms of lost consumer surplus, the average costs per job saved in the agriculture and fisheries sectors (20 million to 41 million won) and

Table 3.4b   Group B: estimated employment effects of removing protection

Sector and product (HS)	Employment before liberalization[a] (thousands of workers)	Loss of employment (thousands of workers)	(percent)	Cost of preserving a job Consumer cost (million won)	Efficiency cost (million won)
Agriculture and fisheries	1,651.9	372.18	22.5	20.2	5.0
Beef (0202)	207.1	32.93	15.9	30.0	10.0
Pork (0203)	161.8	11.26	7.0	16.0	1.0
Poultry (0207)	65.4	5.49	8.4	31.0	15.0
Ivory, antlers, etc. (0507)	1.2	0.08	6.7	131.0	2.0
Dried onions and garlic (0712)	5.2	1.09	21.0	37.0	6.0
Dried beans (0713)	7.8	2.09	26.8	45.0	29.0
Nuts (0802)	14.5	2.75	19.0	35.0	16.0
Bananas (0803)	0.4	0.07	18.0	445.0	36.0
Peppers (0904)	134.7	29.02	21.5	16.0	3.0
Barley (1003)	37.9	9.54	25.2	16.0	3.0
Corn (1005)	3.1	1.23	40.0	544.0	109.0
Milled rice (1006)	869.6	250.20	28.0	15.0	3.0
Malt (1107)	14.9	3.20	21.5	42.0	26.0
Soybeans (1201)	25.8	8.02	31.1	51.0	13.0
Peanuts (1202)	6.6	1.32	20.0	32.0	14.0
Oilseeds (1207)	39.2	10.49	26.8	17.0	3.0
Fish (0301-2)	48.4	3.17	6.5	55.0	4.0
Crabs, lobster and shrimp (0306)	8.3	0.23	2.8	68.0	5.0
Processed foods	114.9	8.51	7.5	176.5	41.1
Dairy products (0401-6)	11.5	2.46	21.4	241.0	49.0
Vegetable extracts (1302)	1.1	0.00	3.0	224.0	9.0
Prepared meat and fish (16)	39.8	2.29	5.8	81.0	8.0
Other sugars (1702)	1.5	0.06	4.0	220.0	36.0
Pasta (1902)	10.8	1.00	9.3	149.0	54.0
Prepared fruits and vegetables (20)	11.4	1.02	8.9	138.0	18.0
Tea and roasted coffee (2101)	2.5	0.10	4.0	277.0	31.0
Sauces and prepared sauces (2103)	7.6	0.25	3.3	157.0	9.0
Other food preparations (2106)	23.7	0.75	3.2	56.0	5.0
Distilled liquor (2208)	4.3	0.36	8.4	519.0	241.0
Leaf tobacco (2401)	1.7	0.22	12.9	520.0	187.0
Minerals and chemical products	9.6	0.47	4.9	138.3	25.5
Natural steatite (2526)	0.4	0.02	5.0	146.0	7.0
Cosmetics (3304)	5.8	0.24	4.1	139.0	24.0
Toilet preparations (3307	0.2	0.01	5.0	261.0	14.0
Casein (3501)	3.2	0.02	6.3	137.0	28.0

(continued)

Table 3.4b (continued)

Sector and product (HS)	Employment before liberalization[a] (thousands of workers)	Loss of employment (thousands of workers)	Loss of employment (percent)	Cost of preserving a job Consumer cost (million won)	Cost of preserving a job Efficiency cost (million won)
Textiles and light industries	269.9	17.73	6.6	33.2	7.0
Plywood (4412)	6.7	0.47	7.0	136.0	11.0
Wooden tableware and kitchenware (4419)	1.2	0.22	18.3	30.0	7.0
Carpets (57)	1.3	0.08	6.2	66.0	6.0
Apparel (61, 62)	225.4	14.41	6.4	29.0	6.0
Other textile articles (63)	23.7	1.82	7.7	43.0	14.0
Porcelain household articles (6911)	9.2	0.58	6.3	23.0	6.0
Glassware (7013)	2.1	0.13	6.2	50.0	4.0
Glass beads and imitation pearls (7018)	0.3	0.02	6.7	216.0	13.0
Machinery and metal products	86.7	5.28	6.1	130.7	18.4
Stoves and ranges (7321)	3.9	0.20	5.1	117.0	28.0
Steel household articles (7323)	17.2	0.88	5.1	38.0	4.0
Aluminum household articles (7615)	3.2	0.17	5.3	49.0	10.0
Motor vehicles for people (8703)	46.7	2.99	6.4	143.0	12.0
Motor vehicles for goods (8704)	15.7	1.04	6.6	190.0	49.0
Miscellaneous goods	6.6	0.59	8.9	81.3	15.3
Electric musical instruments (9207)	0.6	0.05	8.3	184.0	70.0
Equipment for games (9504)	1.0	0.11	11.0	169.0	11.0
Sporting goods (9506)	5.0	0.43	8.6	49.0	13.0
Total for highly protected products	2,138.3	404.76	18.9	25.7	6.1

a. In agriculture, employment for individual commodities is calculated as the number of total agricultural employees multiplied by the production weight for each commodity. Because most Korean farmers raise several different crops and livestock concurrently, employment for individual commodities does not correspond to identifiable farmers raising just that item.

Sources: Korean National Statistical Office 1994; Korean Ministry of Agriculture, Forestry, and Fisheries 1993.

in the textiles and light industries sectors (33 million to 81 million won) are similar to the ranges for protection throughout the Korean economy. However, the costs in the other sectors are much higher. The products that have particularly high costs in preserving each job are in sectors with high capital-labor ratios, such as motor vehicles, machinery and metal products, plywood, and most processed foods and chemical products.

The number of workers displaced by trade liberalization in the 49 sectors does not directly translate into a corresponding increase in unemployment for the economy as a whole. Displaced workers can be and often are employed in more productive sectors through reallocation of the work force. Thus, the cost of shielding a worker in one of the protected sectors from long-term unemployment could be much higher than the levels estimated here.

Comparison with Previous Studies

Comparison with the United States and Japan

This study on the costs of protection in Korea is very similar in methodology, especially in the analytical model, to research on the United States and Japan published by the Institute for International Economics. Unlike those studies, this study does not attempt to quantify nontariff barriers for manufactured goods. But despite the differences in the highly protected sectors and in estimated levels of protection, there are important similarities. Table 3.5 gives side-by-side comparisons for the three studies.

First, protection rates resulting from nontariff barriers are generally much higher than the protection resulting from tariff barriers in all three countries. As a result of several multilateral negotiations under GATT auspices since World War II, import tariffs (the traditional instrument of trade protection) have been steadily reduced to very low levels. In place of tariffs, many countries have used measures such as import quotas and import licensing restrictions on agricultural products; many forms of gray-area measures such as voluntary export restraints (VER) and orderly marketing arrangements (OMA) on textiles and apparel, footwear, steel, and automobiles; and quarantine, labeling, and rules of origin measures to restrict the imports of foreign goods in order to protect specific domestic industries.

Second, in terms of protection levels by sector, the agriculture, fisheries, and textile and apparel sectors are highly protected in all three countries. Tariff equivalents on the agriculture, fisheries, and livestock sectors are estimated to be several hundred percent in both Korea and Japan. In the United States, the tariff equivalents were measured to be as high as 50 to 66 percent (but on products of lesser economic importance).

In Japan, the consumer surplus loss in the foods sector, which has heavy protection, accounted for 53 percent of the total loss in the highly protected sectors in 1989. In Korea, highly protected agriculture and processed foods account for more than 80 percent of the total consumer surplus loss.

Textiles and apparel were also highly protected in all three countries. In the United States, the protection rate on apparel came to 48 percent;

Table 3.5 United States, Japan, and Korea: comparison of protection effects[a]

Country studied (base year)	US (1990)	Japan (1989)	Korea (1992)
Number of sectors (average tariff equivalent)	21 sectors (35%)	47 sectors (178%)	49 sectors (173%)
Selection criteria	• Products with tariffs of 10% or higher, marine transportation, textile and apparel (quotas), selected agricultural products (quotas); • Domestic consumption of US $1.0 billion or more; • Potential benefits of liberalization of US $100 million or more	• Food and beverages and some chemicals with higher tariff equivalents; • Other products with tariff equivalents of 5% or higher; • Import values of 1.0 billion yen or more	• Agricultural and processed foods and manufactured goods with tariffs or tariff equivalents of 12% or higher; • Import values of US$ 10 million or more, plus highly protected agricultural goods.
Characteristics			
Domestic output	US$200 billion (3.6% of GNP)	US$391 billion (7% of GNP)	US$57 billion (18.3% of GNP)
Imports	US$55 billion (10.6% of total)	US$51 billion (19% of total)	US$4 billion (4.9% of total)
Employment	1.8 million workers (1.5% of total)	1.8 million workers (3.2% of total)	2.1 million workers (11.2% of total)
Consumer surplus	US$32.3 billion (0.8% of GNP)	US$75–110 billion (2.6–3.8% of GNP)	US$11.7–13.3 billion (3.8–4.3% of GNP)
Producer surplus	US$15.8 billion	US$65–87 billion	US$8.4–8.9 billion
Tariff revenue	US$5.9 billion	US$2.2 billion	US$0.5 billion
Quota rents	US$7.1 billion	US$20 billion	US$1.3 billion
Efficiency gains	US$3.5 billion	US$17 billion	US$1.0–3.2 billion
Increase in imports	US$16.1 billion	US$53 billion	US$3.7–14.0 billion
Decrease in domestic output	US$16.7 billion	US$33 billion	US$2.8–6.7 billion
Decrease in employment	190,000	182,000	174,000–405,000
Consumer surplus cost per job	US$169,000	US$601,000	US$33,000–67,000
Efficiency cost per job	US$54,000	US$94,000	US$5,000–6,000
(per capita GNP)	(US$22,000)	(US$24,000)	(US$7,000)

on textiles, to 23 percent. Textiles and apparel account for 75 percent of the total consumer surplus loss in the United States. These sectors are protected by high tariffs and quantitative restraints, under the auspices of the Multi-Fiber Arrangements (MFA). Under the Uruguay Round agreement, the MFA will be phased out over 10 years. Tariff-equivalent protection on apparel was estimated to be nearly 300 percent in Japan. Korea, a major exporter of textiles and apparel, also imposed high tariffs on some items in these sectors.

Along with these similarities, the studies of the three countries revealed some marked differences. First, there is a big difference in the industrial and employment structure of the highly protected sectors. The adverse impact of employment decline—one of the costs of trade liberalization—thus differs greatly among the countries. While the share of employment in the highly protected sectors was only 1.5 percent in the United States and 3.2 percent in Japan, it was 11.2 percent in Korea. Sudden trade liberalization in the agricultural sectors of Korea would have severe employment consequences—and it would compel a sharp drop in rural earnings per worker.

Second, because the estimated employment decline in Korea from the removal of protection is so large, the consumer surplus cost per job saved through trade protection in Korea ($33,000 to $67,000) is very low compared with the cost per job in the United States ($169,000) and Japan ($601,000), even allowing for differences in per capita income between the countries. In terms of the efficiency cost per job saved, the figure for Korea is estimated at only $5,000 to $6,000, compared with $54,000 in the United States and $94,000 in Japan.

Comparison with Other Domestic Studies

Recent research on Korea's protection includes the important study *Korea's Industrial Protection and Distortion of Incentive System*, by Jung-ho Yoo et al. (1993). The authors analyze Korea's protection levels by industry in 1990 and estimate the effects of income transfer between sectors as follows:

- The nominal rate of protection, defined as the difference between domestic and c.i.f. import prices in tradeable goods except agriculture, was 22.5 percent in Korea in 1990 (table 2.4). The calculated tariff rate, namely the protection achieved via tariffs, was on average 11.4 percent for all industries (table 2.5). Thus the work of Yoo et al. implies that nontariff barriers amounted to a tariff equivalent of 11 percent on average in 1990.

- The effect of protection in terms of income transferred from consumers to domestic producers in tradeable goods was estimated to amount to 18.0 trillion to 19.4 trillion won. In addition, consumers paid an extra 3.5 trillion won for imported products.

■ Therefore, the total cost to domestic consumers from industrial protection, which Yoo et al. (1993) call an "industrial protection tax," amounted to 21.5 trillion to 22.9 trillion won in 1990. This figure is about twice as large as the 9 trillion to 10 trillion won figure estimated here for highly protected sectors in 1992.

The differences between estimates in Yoo et al. and those in this report mainly reflect differences in the earlier study's calculation of nontariff barriers (NTBs) on tradeable goods (estimated by comparing domestic and c.i.f. import prices), sector coverage, and base year. Yoo et al.'s calculations of nominal protection are based on a large-scale questionnaire survey of individual firms regarding domestic shipment prices of domestic goods on the one hand and import prices of foreign competing goods on the other. This approach implicitly measures nontariff barriers by comparing unit prices of imports and domestic goods, then subtracting the known tariff. According to Yoo et al.'s calculations, NTBs in 1990 were about the same as tariffs on tradeable goods other than agriculture (11 percent in both cases). The additional burden of NTBs accounts for a considerable part of the overall difference between consumer costs estimated by Yoo and those estimated by this study.

Another big difference between the studies is their sector coverage. In Yoo et al., all tradeable goods were considered and 1990 data were used. By contrast, this report uses 1992 data on 49 highly protected products that account for 19 percent of the total tradeable goods in terms of domestic production. It is worth noting that Hufbauer and Elliott (1994) found, for the United States, that consumer losses almost doubled when goods with low levels of protection are taken into account. Returning to Korea, we see that protection in 1990 was somewhat more severe than in 1992: the calculated tariff rate was 10 percent in 1990 versus 6.3 percent in 1992, and the import liberalization ratio was 96.3 percent in 1990 versus 97.7 percent in 1992 (table 2.1).

There are other methodological differences between the two reports. This report uses a partial equilibrium sector-by-sector model, whereas Yoo et al. used a economywide input-output model. In estimating the effects of trade protection, they estimated the effective rate of protection by industry, starting with nominal rates of protection by industry and then translating nominal rates into effective rates by using the input-output coefficient matrix. The authors then estimated the income transfers across sectors that resulted from Korea's overall protective apparatus.

Although many of the estimates of Yoo et al. are not directly comparable to the estimates of this report, the concept of the consumer surplus cost of trade protection used in this report closely resembles the "industrial protection tax" that they calculated.

Limitations of This Report and Future Research Directions

In order to compute the various effects of trade protection in Korea, several assumptions were made. The calculations relied on the assumption that the calculated tariff rates, or tariff equivalents in the case of some items in the agriculture and fisheries sectors and in the processed food industry, could be used to measure the level of protection. Accordingly, the estimated results in the report are subject to a number of limitations. Though its limitations were described in chapter 1, they are restated here to emphasize their importance.

First, NTBs in the manufacturing and service sectors of Korea are an important source of friction between Korea and its trading partners. The difficult task is to estimate the tariff-equivalent level of these NTBs. In this report, the measurement of nontariff protection is limited to certain agricultural goods, where appropriate data are available to compute the level of tariff equivalents. If time and resources were available to contrast domestic and external prices for comparable goods, the price differentials could be used to assess the protection level associated with the presence of nontariff barriers in manufacturing and service sectors, as well as for a broader range of agricultural goods. There have been a number of attempts in the past to collect data item by item for price differentials. However, these attempts were made solely for one-time research purposes, and data collected by the government or industry associations are not made available to the general public in any systematic way.

For the agricultural sector, where some data on domestic and import prices are available, tariff equivalents are calculated on the basis of average price differentials during the period from 1986 to 1988, or during the period from 1986 to 1990. This approach was followed because imports of some items were too small to yield stable or reliable estimates of the protection level in the year 1992 taken alone.

The second key limitation is that the partial equilibrium model is susceptible to important caveats. The effect of protection measured under this approach is limited, in the sense that it captures the impact only on the protected industry and its consumers. The calculations do not include indirect impacts on other industries or other countries. In order to assess these broader effects, the linkage among industries would need to be examined (using, for example, an input-output table), and trade relations with other countries would need to be modeled in a computable general equilibrium framework. Those tasks were beyond the resources available for this project.

Third, in order to measure the effect of protection precisely, specific elasticity parameters would be needed to reflect Korean economic conditions. Because of the lack of data, this report used assumed ranges of elasticities for groups of similar products. In setting the assumed range of elasticities, previous studies and theoretical considerations were taken into account. Despite the wide ranges of elasticities selected in this report, the ranges of the calculated welfare effects are not so great.

Fourth, this study is confined to the 49 products that met the conditions of having higher than 12 percent tariff-equivalent protection and exceeding $10 million of imports (plus certain highly protected agricultural goods). Future studies should attempt to cover *all* trade in goods and services.

Conclusions

The findings in this report carry with them several policy implications. Trade protection and other restrictive regulations need to be progressively removed. Price distortions caused by trade protection hinder the efficient allocation of economic resources and reduce national welfare. Excessive government regulation conflicts with the worldwide movement toward deregulation and globalization.

Lowering tariff rates and removing quantitative restrictions are necessary but not sufficient to liberalize trade. These measures should be complemented with government efforts to abolish entry barriers to all economic activities, efforts to improve distribution practices, and efforts to increase transparency in administrative procedures. The government should focus on enhancing market competition to make the Korean business environment more dynamic.

Appendix A
Measuring the Costs of Korea's Visible Trade Protection in 1992: The Methodology

The Computable Partial Equilibrium Model

In order to simulate the potential scenario in which protection is eliminated, use is made of the computable partial equilibrium model developed by Peter Uimonen in Hufbauer and Elliott (1994). The framework is similar to that found in Morkre and Tarr (1980) and Tarr and Morkre (1984). It is founded on a partial equilibrium analysis with four key assumptions:

- The domestic good and the imported good are imperfect substitutes.

- The supply schedule for the imported good is flat (perfectly elastic).

- The supply schedule for the domestic good is upwardly sloped (less than perfectly elastic).

- All markets are perfectly competitive.

The effects of removing a trade barrier (either a tariff or a quota) are illustrated in figures A.1 and A.2. For example, elimination of a tariff lowers the price of the import in the domestic market from Pm to Pm' in figure A.1. In figure A.2, the decrease in the price of the imported good causes an inward shift in the demand curve for the domestic commodity from Dd to Dd'. This in turn leads to a decrease in the price of the domestic product from Pd to Pd'.

Returning to figure A.1, we see that the decrease in the domestic price causes the demand schedule for the imported good to shift inward from Dm to Dm'. When equilibrium is restored, prices of both the imported

Figure A.1   Effects in the import market of removing a trade barrier

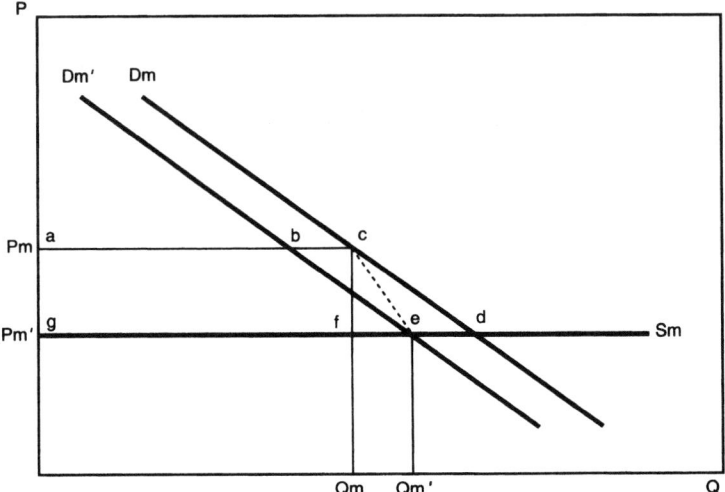

With the trade barrier in place, the price of the import in the protected market is *Pm*, and the quantity imported is *Qm*. Following liberalization, the price falls to *Pm'*, the world price. Then, responding to a lower price in the domestic market (see figure A.2), the demand schedule for the import shifts from *Dm* to *Dm'*, and the quanity imported settles at *Qm'*.

Figure A.2   Effects in the domestic market of removing a trade barrier

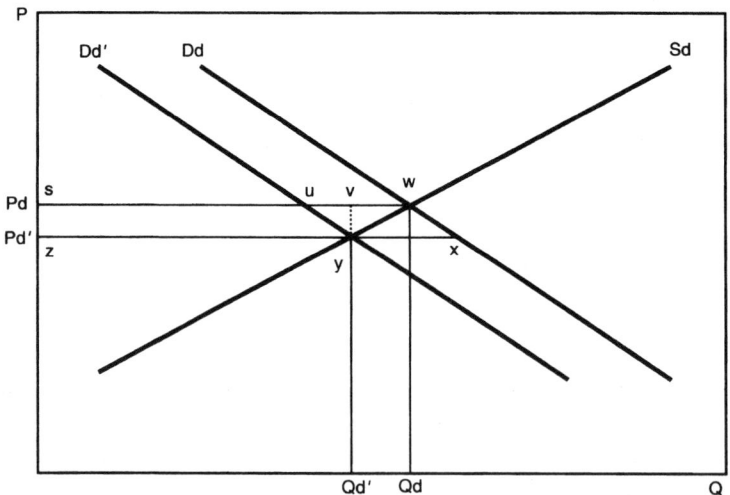

With the trade barrier in place, the price of the import-competing domestic product is *Pd*, and the quantity demanded is *Qd*. Following liberalization and the decline in the import price (see figure A.1), demand for the domestic substitute falls, shifting the demand curve from *Dd* to *Dd'*, the quantity consumed falls to *Qd'*, and the price drops to *Pd'*.

good and domestic good are lower, output of the domestically produced good is also lower (by the difference between Qd to Qd' shown in figure A.2), and the quantity of imports is higher (by the difference between Qm to Qm' in figure A.1).[1]

With the trade barrier in place, the price of the import in the protected market is Pm, and the quantity imported is Qm. Following liberalization, the price falls to Pm', the world price. Then, responding to a lower price in the domestic market (figure A.2), the demand schedule for the import shifts from Dm to Dm', and the quantity imported settles at Qm'. With the trade barrier in place, the price of the import-competing domestic product is Pd, and the quantity demanded is Qd. Following liberalization and the decline in the import price (figure A.1), demand for the domestic substitute falls, shifting the demand curve from Dd to Dd'; the quantity consumed falls to Qd'; and the price drops to Pd'.

Calculating the Welfare Effects of Trade Barriers

The changes in prices and quantities due to trade liberalization result in a gain of consumer surplus, both in the import market and in the domestic market. Most of the gain arises because consumers now pay less for a good than they paid when supply was restricted. In addition, some potential consumers were previously priced out of the market entirely, and they now become purchasers at the lower price. The consumer surplus gain in the domestic market resulting from trade liberalization totally offsets the loss of producer surplus experienced by domestic firms as prices and output both fall.

If the trade restraint took the form of a tariff, then the revenue lost by the government would partially offset the consumer gain in the market for imported goods. If, instead, a quantitative restraint (QR) was used, liberalization would eliminate the quota rents that previously went either to domestic importers or to foreign exporters, or to some combination of the two, depending both on how the QR was allocated and on the economic power of the market participants (see Bergsten et al. 1987). Finally, there will be an efficiency gain because the trade restraint resulted in a misallocation of resources. Before liberalization, the wedge created between the domestic price of the import and the world price caused a transfer of resources toward production of the import substitute and away from other sectors where those resources could have been used more efficiently.

The methodology used here to quantify these welfare effects is based on Morkre and Tarr (1980). Morkre and Tarr estimate that the consumer

---

1. The same story could be told if the initial liberalization measure were to increase an import quota from Qm to Qm'. Then the system would work back to lower import prices.

surplus gain from liberalization in the import market is approximated—if we return to figure A.1—by the area bounded by points *aceg*. This method of estimating the consumer gain in the import market follows from the analysis of Burns (1973) and gives an average of the consumer gains calculated separately from the two demand curves.[2] Using the old demand schedule *(Dm)* gives the area marked *acdg* as the change in consumer surplus, while the new demand schedule *(Dm')* gives the area marked *abeg*. The difference between the two areas is shown by the parallelogram marked *bcde*. Line *ce* divides the area in half and gives the compromise consumer surplus change, area *aceg*. Area *aceg* can be estimated by adding rectangle *acfg* to triangle *cef*.

If the form of the protection is a tariff, the rectangular area *acfg* represents a transfer from the government to consumers in the form of lost tariff revenues, which may be estimated as:

$$(Pm - Pm') \times (Qm) \tag{A.1}$$

The area of the triangle marked *cef* represents recovery of the deadweight efficiency loss, which may be estimated as:

$$(1/2) \times [((Pm - Pm') \times (Qm' - Qm)] \tag{A.2}$$

If quantitative restraints are used, and if all the quota rents were previously captured by foreign exporters, then area *acfg* is recovered by the domestic economy from foreign quota holders. In that case, the consumer gain in the import market, the sum of rectangle *acfg* and triangle *cef*, will also equal the net national welfare gain. If both tariffs and quotas are imposed, the tariff equivalent of the quota is assumed to be the difference between the total decline in the import price *(Pm − Pm')* and the price effect of the tariff.[3] To the extent that the tariff equivalent of the quota is recovered from foreign quota holders, there will be a gain to the domestic economy.

Turning next to the domestic effects in figure A.2, we see that the consumer welfare gain from lower domestic prices may be approximated by the area marked *swyz*. Area *swyz* can be estimated by adding rectangle *svyz* and triangle *vwy*. This amounts to:

$$(Pd - Pd') \times (Qd') + (1/2) \times [(Pd - Pd') \times (Qd - Qd')] \tag{A.3}$$

In the domestic market, the consumer surplus gain is just offset by the producer surplus loss.

Applying the Model

In order to apply the analysis to particular cases, a simple computable equilibrium model was devised corresponding to the graphical analysis

---

2. See Jones (1993) for a mathematical proof of the validity of this method.

3. The price effect of the tariff is normally calculated as *Pm'* times the ad valorem tariff rate. The same approach is used here.

above. The form of the model chosen assumes that demand and supply relationships are linear not in absolute terms but in terms of their logarithms. This assumption enables the parameters associated with the price terms to be interpreted as elasticities.

In order to achieve this result, it is necessary to specify the underlying domestic demand and supply functions according to the following forms:

$$Qd = aPd^{Edd}Pm^{Edm} \tag{A.4}$$

$$Qs = bPd^{Es} \tag{A.5}$$

In equation A.4, *Edd* is the own-price elasticity of demand for the domestic commodity, while *Edm* is the cross-price elasticity of demand for the domestic commodity with respect to the price of the imported commodity.[4] In equation A.5, *Es* is the own-price elasticity of the supply of the domestic good. Since the domestic commodity and the import are imperfect substitutes in this model, equilibrium in the domestic market requires that domestic demand equals domestic supply: in other words, that *Qd* equals *Qs*.

Assuming that the supply of the imports is perfectly elastic, the supply and demand equations in the import market are:

$$Qm = cPd^{Emd}Pm^{Emm} \tag{A.6}$$

$$Pm = Pm'(1+t) \tag{A.7}$$

In equation A.6, *Emd* is the cross-price elasticity of demand for the imported commodity with respect to the price of the domestic commodity, while *Emm* is the own-price elasticity of demand for the imported commodity. Equation A.7 represents the assumption that the supply of the imported commodity is perfectly elastic, and therefore that the world price, *Pm'*, which equals *Pm*/(1 + t), is the same no matter what the level of imports.

This system of demand and supply functions may be transformed into a system of linear relationships simply by taking the logarithms to the base *e* (shown by ln) of equations A.4, A.5, A.6, and A.7:

$$\ln Qd = \ln a + Edd\ln Pd + Edm\ln Pm \tag{A.8}$$

$$\ln Qs = \ln b + Es\ln Pd \tag{A.9}$$

---

4. The own-price elasticity of demand for the domestic commodity, *Edd*, is defined as the percentage change in the quantity demanded for each 1 percent change in the price. Other own-price elasticities are defined in an analogous way. Own-price elasticities are normally negative (e.g., a fall in price creates an increase in demand for the domestic good). The cross-price elasticity of demand for the domestic commodity, *Edm*, is defined as the percentage change in the quantity of the domestic good demanded for each 1 percent change in the price of the imported good. Other cross-price elasticities are defined in a similar way. Cross-price elasticities are normally positive (e.g., an increase in the price of the imported good causes an increase in demand for the domestic good).

$$\ln Qm = \ln c + Emd\ln Pd + Emm\ln Pm \qquad (A.10)$$

$$\ln Pm = \ln[Pm'(1 + t)] \qquad (A.11)$$

Estimating the effects of a change in trade protection using this system requires two basic steps. First, price and quantity data are used, together with estimates of the elasticity parameters, to solve equations A.8, A.9, and A.10 for the constant terms, namely $\ln a$, $\ln b$, and $\ln c$. These terms represent the effects of unobserved nonprice variables on the demand and supply functions. The crucial assumption in this step is that the base period for which the price and quantity data are collected may be considered an equilibrium period.

The second step is to use the estimates of the intercepts and the elasticity parameters, together with a separately estimated change in either the price or the quantity of the import due to a change in protection, to calculate a new equilibrium and, hence, the comparative-static welfare effects of the change.

Suppose, for example, that a tariff is eliminated. By invoking the assumption that $\ln Qd$ equals $\ln Qs$, equations A.8 and A.9 may be solved together to yield the new price of the domestic commodity as a function of the new import price:

$$\ln Pd' = [(\ln a - \ln b)/(Es - Edd)] + [Edm/(Es - Edd)] \times \ln Pm' \quad (A.12)$$

In equation A.12, Pm' equals the previous (base period) import price (corresponding to Pm in figure A.1) minus the change in the price induced by elimination of the tariff (corresponding to the difference between Pm and Pm' in figure A.1). To facilitate computation, base period prices (inclusive of the tariff) are assumed equal to index values of 1.00. Tariff changes are expressed in ad valorem terms where the ad valorem rate is applied to the world price without the tariff, Pm'. For example, elimination of a 15 percent tariff would mean that Pm' is equal to (0.87), i.e., to (1/1.15). The new import and domestic prices can then be substituted into equations A.8, A.9, and A.10 to yield the new equilibrium quantities of imports and domestic output. The welfare effects of the tariff change may then be computed using expressions A.1, A.2, and A.3.

In many Korean agricultural markets, quantitative restrictions have been in place for a very long period. Often it is possible to estimate the price effect of the quota using data on prices in the world and domestic markets. This estimated "tariff equivalent" of the quota (plus any tariff that is imposed) may then be used to calculate Pm', which in turn is inserted into equation A.12 and used to calculate the other prices and quantities, as in the pure tariff case.

Statistical Data and Elasticities

Statistical Data

In estimating the effects of trade protection using the model presented in the previous section, several data observations are necessary:

- data on the four variables Qd, Qm, Pd, and Pm for the 49 sectors with high trade protection in 1992;

- collected tariff rates (t) or tariff equivalents of quotas on agricultural products $(t.e.)$, and elasticities (Edd, Edm, Emd, Emm, and Es), to estimate the new equilibrium (Qd', Qm', Pd', and Pm') after removing trade protection;

- the base level of employment (Ld) in 1992, to estimate the effect on employment in the protected sector. Employment is assumed to decrease by the percentage drop in domestic production.

The following sources were used:

- for Qd, Pd, and Ld, the *Report on Mining and Manufacturing Survey 1992*, published by Korea's National Statistical Office in 1994, and the *Statistical Yearbook of Agriculture, Forestry, and Fisheries 1992*, published by Korea's Ministry of Agriculture, Forestry, and Fisheries in 1993;

- for Qm, Pm, and t, the *Statistical Yearbook of Foreign Trade 1992*, published by the Office of Customs Administration, and data on Korea's foreign trade and tariffs, which were also compiled by the Office of Customs Administration;

- for $t.e.$, *Review of the Uruguay Round Text on Agriculture and Policy Implications*, by Korea's Economic Planning Board, and *Uruguay Round Schedule LX — Republic of Korea, Agricultural Products* (March 1994).

The 1992 collected tariff rates and the commodity classification by Harmonized System (HS) code were chosen for a number of reasons.

First, 1992 was chosen as the base year because this is the most recent year for which data on industrial production and employment are available.

Second, collected tariff rates are used instead of statutory tariff rates because, owing to flexible tariffs and tariff abatement systems, statutory rates are not always applied. Even if they were applied, the statutory rates would differ among individual items within the same product group. The collected tariff rates can be considered the import-weighted average of the different applied tariffs within each product group. Because high tariffs depress imports, an import-weighted tariff average is biased downward in comparison to a production-weighted tariff average (box A.1).

Third, the HS code carries a certain advantage in classifying products. It is easy to gather recent data on trade volumes and the collected tariff rates by using the HS code. However, this information must then be matched with the Korean Standard Industrial Classification (KSIC) system. The HS classifies items by product characteristics for trade and tariff-related purposes. The KSIC classifies items by characteristics of

Box A.1 A note on measuring average protection levels

This study measures protection rates for a variety of sectors. For most of these sectors, what is measured is solely visible, tariff rate protection. In agricultural sectors only, additional estimates for the tariff equivalent of non-tariff barriers are made.

The basic, collected tariff rate of a given sector i is calculated as:

$$t_i = \frac{\text{tariff revenue}}{\text{import value}}$$

In this simple case, the t_i value amounts to an import-weighted average of collected tariff rates for individual items. This method applies to the lion's share of trade protection calculations made in this study.

In the case of most agricultural sectors, the starting point was an estimate of the tariff equivalent of both tariff and nontariff barriers. When the sector comprises of several items (expressed as $j = 1, \ldots n$), each with different tariff equivalents, then the tariff equivalent of total protection is calculated as follows:

$$TE_i = \sum_{j=1}^{n} W_j \, TE_j$$

In this case, W_j is the *domestic production weight* of item j in sector i, and TE_j is the tariff equivalent of total protection of item j. The reason for domestic production weights is simple: due to heavy protection, there are very small imports of important products such as milled rice and pork, making import weights inappropriate.

The tariff equivalent of the nontariff barrier alone is calculated by subtracting the average collected tariff rate from the tariff equivalent of total protection ($NTB_i = TE_i - t_i$).

In the agricultural sectors where nontariff barriers were calculated, the level of overall protection is domestic-production-weighted, not import-weighted. Since collected tariffs are generally low, this in turn implies that nontariff barrier estimates are predominantly production-weighted.

---

employment and the production process. The concordance used to match the HS with the KSIC is presented in table A.8. The concordance is a first approximation and will require further work in the future.

An alternative procedure would have been to use the *1990 Input-Output Table* and its "Supporting Tables on Domestic Products and Imports by Sector and Commodity" published by the Bank of Korea in 1993. This approach would have enabled the calculation of a price differential for each item. These price differentials might then be characterized as tariff-equivalent measures of Korean protection. However, this approach would entail the controversies and difficulties of unit value comparisons. Moreover, given the rapid changes in the industrial structure and recent market-opening measures in Korea, it seemed better to focus on 1992 experience rather than on 1990 experience.

The 106 highly protected items in the 49 highly protected sectors constitute 8.7 percent of the 1,214 total items in the four-digit HS. The import value of these items in 1992 amounted to 3.1 trillion won on a c.i.f. basis (US$3.98 billion), or approximately 5 percent of Korea's total imports. Domestic output in these sectors equaled 44.7 trillion won (US$57.2 billion), or 18 percent of output in all the tradeable sectors (agriculture, forestry, fisheries, mining, and manufactures).

Among the protected sectors, the imports of agriculture and fisheries amounted to 1.6 trillion won, about half of total imports of highly protected products. This was followed by processed foods (477 billion won), textiles and light industries (588 billion won), and machinery and metal products (175 billion won). The domestic output from these protected sectors, expressed as a percent of total value of protected sectors, came mainly from agriculture and fisheries (31 percent), machinery and metal products (26 percent), processed foods (20 percent), and textiles and light industries (20 percent). The dominant individual products were motor vehicles (17 percent of highly protected production), textiles (16 percent), and rice (15 percent).

The average collected tariff rate for these products in 1992 was 16.8 percent. The highest rates were on bananas (85 percent), followed by agriculture and fishery products such as dried onions and garlic (53 percent), live and fresh fish (47 percent), peanuts (40 percent), and peppers (39 percent); they were also high on processed foods such as pasta (45 percent) and prepared fruits and vegetables (43 percent). The lowest tariff rates were on corn (3 percent), soybeans (3 percent), and rice (5 percent). In 1992, the average collected tariff rate of items not covered on the list of highly protected products was 5.8 percent, and the average collected tariff rate on total Korean imports was 6.3 percent.

Measured by the tariff equivalent of total trade barriers—both tariff and nontariff—protection levels for important agricultural products ranged from 51 percent (pork) to 595 percent (rice).[5]

Depending on data availability, different methods were used to calculate tariff-equivalent levels for different products. The tariff-equivalent levels for potatoes, barley, soybeans, red beans, green beans, and peanuts are the base rates for tariff reduction as presented in the Korea's Country Schedule annexed to the Uruguay Round agreement for tariffication of items with nontariff barriers. The tariff-equivalent levels for beef, pork, poultry, and rice are the price differentials between domestic and foreign goods for the period of 1986-90, as presented in the report of the Economic

---

5. Protection is probably not the sole reason for price differentials between domestic and foreign prices. However, we can conclude that the differentials mainly reflect protection of these items, since the Korean government (among other institutions) established the protection levels after calculating price differentials (taking into account product quality differences) for 1986-88 or 1986-90.

Planning Board. The levels for dairy products (such as milk powder and milk whey), dried onions and garlic, peppers, and sesame were calculated from the ceiling binding tariff rates and the base tariff rates specified in the Uruguay Round Country Schedule. The overall tariff-equivalent levels for four-digit HS products comprising several subdivided items with different rates were calculated by taking the weighted average of individual tariff equivalents, using as weights the value of domestic production.

Elasticity Estimation and Assumptions

This analysis uses elasticities estimated in other studies, rather than embarking on a fresh attempt at estimation. To determine the range of elasticity values to apply to each product group, elasticities used by the Korea Rural Economic Institute, as well as those used in studies of protection in the United States and Japan, are taken into account (table A.9).

It would have been desirable to estimate the elasticities pertinent to each item to reflect the specific characteristics of the Korean economy. However, that task was beyond the resources available. Moreover, since Korea's economic structures of production, consumption, and imports have changed dramatically during the last two to three decades, stable data sets required for estimating elasticities are largely unavailable. In addition, for rice, barley, and pork, elasticities are almost impossible to estimate, since insignificant imports mean that data on import prices and volumes are not reliable. Likewise, meaningful analysis is hard to undertake for products such as automobiles, where only in recent years have domestic output and imports increased rapidly.

There is a final obstacle. Economic performance under a trading regime with little or no distortion would be most useful for estimating the various price elasticities. However, data are only available for periods in which Korean imports were prohibited or severely restrained.

Thus this analysis uses a relatively wide range of elasticity values, drawn from other sources for each product group. Consequently, protection effects are estimated for ranges rather than as point values.

Assumed Ranges of Demand Elasticities

The own-price elasticities of demand for a good (Edd and Emm) represent how demand for the good responds to changes in its price. Economic theory and empirical observation both suggest that own-price demand elasticities are influenced by a number of product characteristics.

For instance, the levels of Edd and Emm depend on the existence of close substitutes for the product in question and on the degree of substitutability between these goods. Korean "necessities," such as rice and peppers, have few substitutes. Hence, the demand for such products is not greatly affected by changes in their prices. For products like these, with few substitutes, the own-price elasticity of demand is expected to be low. The converse would be true for products with a wide range of substitutes.

The precision with which a good is defined also affects the estimate of its price elasticity. Narrowly defined items, such as "automobiles with a cylinder capacity of 1800 cc," will have more substitutes than broadly defined ones, such as "transportation equipment." Thus, the price elasticity of demand for the former will be higher than for the latter.

In setting the assumed ranges of demand elasticities, three steps are followed:

- For each product, a reasonable range of values for either Edd or Emm is determined, based upon economic theory and previous research results.

- When using an assumed range of values for Edd, Emm is then calculated using a conversion factor. Alternatively, when an assumed range is used for Emm, Edd is then calculated using a similar conversion factor.

- The cross elasticities of demand, Emd and Edm, are calculated by multiplying Emm and Edd by a conversion factor of 0.7.

These steps are discussed in greater detail below.

Assuming a Range of Values for Edd or Emm For each product, a range of values is assumed for either Edd or Emm. If the value of domestic production of the product (Vd) is larger than the value of its imports (Vm), a range of values is assumed for Edd. Conversely, if Vm is larger than Vd, a range of values is assumed for Emm. Since Vm is larger than Vd for only 5 of the 49 products, a range of values was assumed for Edd in most cases.

The following ranges apply:

- -0.20 to -0.50 for agricultural and fisheries products;

- -0.30 to -0.75 for processed foods;

- -0.40 to -1.00 for mineral and chemical products;

- -0.50 to -1.25 for machinery and metal products;

- -0.50 to -1.50 for textiles and light industries;

- -0.50 to -2.00 for miscellaneous manufactured goods.

Calculating Emm or Edd Next, the assumed ranges of Edd (or Emm) are used to calculate Emm (or Edd). This is done through the use of the approximation relationship derived by Rousslang and Suomela (1985, 83) and USITC (1989, D-3):

$$Emm = Vd/Vm \times Edd \tag{A.13}$$

$$Edd = Vm/Vd \times Emm \qquad\qquad\qquad (A.14)$$

where Vm is the landed value of imports, including any duty, and Vd is the value of domestic production.

These approximation rules are modified by two constraints that are invoked to avoid unrealistic results. The first constraint is necessitated by the fact that the Vd/Vm ratio is very high for some Korean products (for the heavily protected milled rice product category, the ratio is 16,808!). Simply using the approximation rule, therefore, would result in unrealistically high elasticities. To overcome this problem, an upper limit of 15 is invoked for the ratio Vd/Vm or Vm/Vd. In effect, the cap of 15 constrains all own-price elasticities to be less in absolute value than 30, since the highest assumed own-price elasticity in the ranges detailed earlier has an absolute value of 2.

The second constraint is applied because the unusually high protection levels and Vd/Vm ratios on some products can result in unrealistic solution values. To avoid this problem, the absolute values of Emm (or Edd) are raised to levels such that postliberalization consumption quantities (imports plus domestic production) of the product are greater than or equal to preliberalization consumption:

$$Qm' + Qd' \geq Qm + Qd \qquad\qquad\qquad (A.15)$$

This constraint is similar to the law of demand for normal goods, which posits that the total consumption of a good should increase when its price falls (in this case, through import liberalization). The main difference, of course, is that the imported good and the domestically produced good are imperfect substitutes. Strictly speaking, therefore, adding together domestically produced goods with imported goods is like adding apples and oranges. Hence the constraint (equation A.15) should only be interpreted as a rough indicator of erroneously low Emm or Edd values.

Some of the own-price elasticities of import demand that are derived using this procedure reach the range of 20 to 25 in absolute value. These may seem like high values, but it is important to remember that these are not long-run equilibrium elasticities for a totally liberalized market. Instead, they reflect the initial surge in demand when a highly restricted market with very few imports is deregulated.

Calculation of Edm and Emd   Based upon empirical evidence from Hufbauer and Elliott (1994), the cross-price demand elasticities, Edm and Emd, are calculated at 70 percent of the absolute values of Edd and Emm, respectively.[6]

---

6. The factor of 0.7 is based on the demand elasticity calculations for the US economy in Hufbauer and Elliott (1994). In their study, the average value of the ratio of the cross-price demand elasticities to the own-price demand elasticities was 0.76.

Assumed Range of Supply Elasticities

The price elasticity of supply (Es) for a good represents how domestic output changes in response to changes in its price. We know that supply elasticities, like demand elasticities, are influenced by a number of product characteristics. Supply elasticities are high for products whose supply can be easily adjusted by changing the amount of labor inputs, since workers can be hired or laid off in the short run. By contrast, goods that must be produced using huge fixed facilities and requiring large amounts of capital generally have low supply elasticities.

Es values for each sector are set as follows:

■ 0.20 to 0.50 for agriculture and fish, with a long period of production and rigidity in the input mix;

■ 0.30 to 0.75 for processed foods, with a high degree of dependence on the domestic supply conditions of agricultural and fisheries products;

■ 0.40 to 1.00 for minerals and chemical products;

■ 0.50 to 1.25 for machinery and metal products;

■ 0.50 to 1.50 for textiles and light industrial products;

■ 0.50 to 2.00 for miscellaneous manufactured goods.

Appendix Table A.1 Korea's legal tariff rate structure by commodity group

HS	Number of 4-digit items	Description	1992			1994		
			Low	High	Avg.	Low	High	Avg.
01	13	Live animals	0	20	11.8	0	20	11.1
02	10	Meat and edible meat offal	4	50	29.4	3	50	29.3
03	15	Fish and crustaceans	10	20	16.7	10	20	16.7
04	13	Dairy produce, birds' eggs, etc.	11	40	31.6	8	40	31.4
05	30	Products of animal origin, n.e.s.	0	30	8.7	0	30	6.7
06	9	Live trees and other plants	11	30	13.1	8	25	9.9
07	30	Edible vegetables	0	50	30.6	0	50	30.5
08	35	Edible fruits and nuts	30	50	42.1	30	50	38.0
09	20	Coffee, tea, and spices	4	50	15.0	3	50	12.4
10	10	Cereals	0	35	7.1	0	30	6.2
11	9	Milling industry products	9	35	12.8	5	30	9.1
12	42	Oil seeds and oleaginous fruits	0	40	9.8	0	40	8.9
13	15	Lacs, gums, and resins	10	35	10.8	3	30	8.6
14	14	Vegetable plaiting materials	4	11	5.8	3	8	4.2
15	45	Animal or vegetable fats	4	40	13.0	3	40	10.8
16	5	Preparations of meat, fish, or crustaceans	20	30	26.0	20	30	26.0
17	15	Sugars and sugar confectionery	4	20	11.1	3	20	8.7
18	15	Cocoa and cocoa preparations	4	13	10.4	3	8	7.7
19	13	Preparations of cereals, flour	11	40	17.5	8	40	14.6
20	25	Preparations of vegetables, fruits, and nuts	11	50	39.0	8	50	37.9
21	13	Miscellaneous edible preparations	11	40	16.1	8	40	12.2
22	12	Beverages, spirits, and vinegar	11	40	27.7	8	30	20.8
23	22	Residues and waste from the food industries	5	9	5.7	5	5	5.0
24	6	Tobacco and tobacco substitutes	20	40	36.7	20	40	36.7
25	93	Salt, sulfur, earth, and stone	1	11	4.5	1	8	3.3
26	56	Ores, slag, and ash	1	2	1.3	1	2	1.3
27	61	Mineral fuels	1	11	4.9	1	8	4.6
28	107	Inorganic chemicals	0	11	8.7	0	8	6.5
29	317	Organic chemicals	5	11	10.2	5	8	7.8
30	23	Pharmaceutical products	0	11	4.3	0	8	3.1
31	11	Fertilizers	1	11	6.2	1	8	4.8
32	20	Tanning or dyeing extracts	10	11	11.0	8	8	8.0
33	12	Essential oils and resinoids	11	13	12.0	8	8	8.0
34	10	Soap, organic surface-active agents	11	13	11.2	8	8	8.0
35	9	Albuminoidal substances	11	20	12.0	8	20	9.3
36	6	Explosives, pyrotechnic products, etc.	11	11	11.0	8	8	8.0
37	32	Photographic or cinematographic goods	0	11	7.4	0	8	5.5

Appendix Table A.1 (continued)

HS	Number of 4-digit items	Description	1992			1994		
			Low	High	Avg.	Low	High	Avg.
38	48	Miscellaneous chemical products	5	11	10.5	5	8	7.9
39	39	Plastics and plastic articles	10	11	10.9	8	8	8.0
40	34	Rubber and rubber articles	2	11	8.6	2	8	6.6
41	20	Raw hides or skins and leather	4	11	5.9	3	8	3.9
42	6	Articles of leather, etc.	11	13	12.3	8	8	8.0
43	12	Furskins and artificial fur	4	13	5.8	3	8	4.0
44	72	Wood and articles of wood	2	11	7.1	2	8	4.6
45	4	Cork and articles of cork	11	11	11.0	8	8	8.0
46	6	Straw or esparto products	10	11	10.8	8	8	8.0
47	23	Wood pulp	2	2	2.0	2	2	2.0
48	28	Paper and paperboard	10	13	10.6	8	8	8.0
49	27	Printed books, newspapers, etc.	0	13	1.7	0	8	0.3
50	14	Silk	2	11	5.2	2	8	4.1
51	32	Wool, fine or coarse animal hair	2	11	4.3	2	8	3.5
52	14	Cotton	2	11	7.8	2	8	5.9
53	26	Other vegetable textile fibers	2	11	4.1	2	8	3.4
54	8	Man-made filaments	11	11	11.0	8	8	8.0
55	16	Man-made staple fibers	2	11	10.4	2	8	7.6
56	12	Wadding, felt and nonwovens	10	11	10.9	8	8	8.0
57	5	Carpets	11	13	12.6	8	8	8.0
58	11	Special woven fabrics	11	13	11.2	8	8	8.0
59	11	Coated, covered, or laminated textile fabrics	11	11	11.0	8	8	8.0
60	2	Knitted or crocheted fabrics	11	11	11.0	8	8	8.0
61	17	Articles of apparel knitted or crocheted	13	13	13.0	8	8	8.0
62	17	Articles of apparel not knitted or crocheted	13	13	13.0	8	8	8.0
63	10	Other made-up textile articles	11	11	11.0	8	8	8.0
64	6	Footwear, gaiters, etc.	11	11	11.0	8	8	8.0
65	7	Headgear and headgear parts	11	11	11.0	8	8	8.0
66	3	Umbrellas, parasols, and walking sticks	11	11	11.0	8	8	8.0
67	4	Prepared feathers and down	11	11	11.0	8	8	8.0
68	15	Articles of stone, plaster, and cement	11	11	11.0	8	8	8.0
69	14	Ceramic products	11	13	11.7	8	8	8.0
70	24	Glass and glassware	4	13	10.8	3	8	7.7
71	44	Natural or cultured pearls and stones	0	11	5.5	0	8	4.0
72	59	Iron and steel	2	10	6.3	2	8	5.4
73	28	Articles of iron or steel	10	13	11.2	8	8	8.0
74	38	Cooper and copper articles	2	13	10.1	1	8	7.2
75	10	Nickel and nickel articles	2	11	7.1	1	8	5.5

Appendix Table A.1   (continued)

HS	Number of 4-digit items	Description	1992			1994		
			Low	High	Avg.	Low	High	Avg.
76	18	Aluminum and aluminum articles	2	13	9.6	1	8	7.4
78	9	Lead and lead articles	2	11	8.6	1	8	5.7
79	7	Zinc and zinc articles	2	11	9.4	1	8	6.6
80	7	Tin and tin articles	2	11	9.4	1	8	6.6
81	35	Other base metals and cermets	2	11	6.8	1	8	5.4
82	15	Tools and implements of base metal	11	11	11.0	8	8	8.0
83	20	Miscellaneous articles of base metal	10	13	11.0	8	8	8.0
84	228	Nuclear reactors, machinery, and mechanical appliances	0	13	10.4	0	8	7.6
85	113	Electrical machinery and equipment	5	13	10.9	5	8	7.8
86	28	Railway or tramway locomotives	5	11	5.4	5	8	5.2
87	32	Vehicles other than railway	0	17	11.2	0	10	7.4
88	33	Aircraft and spacecraft	0	11	1.8	0	8	1.5
89	27	Ships, boats, and floating structures	0	11	3.4	0	8	3.3
90	58	Optical or surgical instruments and apparatus	10	13	11.2	8	8	8.0
91	36	Clocks and watches	11	13	11.6	8	8	8.0
92	9	Musical instruments	11	13	11.2	8	8	8.0
93	22	Arms and ammunition	0	13	5.9	0	8	4.0
94	6	Furniture and bedding	11	11	11.0	8	8	8.0
95	8	Toys and sports goods	11	13	11.5	8	8	8.0
96	18	Miscellaneous manufactured goods	11	13	11.1	8	8	8.0
97	12	Works of art and antiques	0	0	0.0	0	0	0.0
Total	2,700		0	50	10.1	0	50	7.9

Appendix Table A.2 Items under flexible tariff system: adjustment tariffs

Code of Korea	Description	Tariff rate[a] (percent)	Period
0301	Tropical fish, true bass, sting, sea bass, loaches	100	1/93–12/94
0706	Carrots	100	1/93–12/93
0709	Fresh oak mushrooms and bracken	100	1/93–12/94
0710	Frozen bracken	100	1/93–12/94
0711	Bracken	100	1/93–12/94
0712	Dried oak mushrooms and radishes	100/60	1/93–12/94
0813	Persimmons	100	1/93–12/94
0901	Coffee and coffee substitutes containing coffee	10	1/94–12/94
1212	Seaweed	70	1/94– 3/95
1605	Bai top shell	100	1/93–12/94
1701	Sugar	60	1/94–12/94
1704	Sugar confectionery	27	1/93–12/93
1806	Food preparation containing cocoa	27	1/93–12/93
1902	Chinese vermicelli	60	1/92–12/94
2101	Extracts, essences, and concentrates of coffee	10	1/91–12/91
2103	Maejoo, mixed seasonings	60	1/93– 3/95
2106	Acorn flour	60	1/93–12/93
2308	Acorns	100	1/93–12/93
3920	Film of plastics	30	1/93–12/94
4402	Wood charcoal	11	1/93–12/93
4408	Veneer sheets	51	1/93–12/93
4409	Rounded wooden sticks	51/50	1/93–12/94
4412	Plywood (thickness not less than 6 mm)	15	1/92–12/94
4419	Wood chopsticks	33	10/91–12/94
4421	Wood fans	100	1/93–12/93
	Toothpicks	51	1/93–12/93
4601	Mats	100	1/93–12/94
5002	Raw silk (not more than 20 decitex)	50	1/94–12/94
5111	Woven fabrics of carded wool	19	1/94–12/94
5112	Woven fabrics of combed wool	19	1/94–12/94
5208	Woven fabrics of cotton	40	1/93–12/94
5515	Woven fabrics of synthetic staple fibers	19	1/94–12/94
5803	Gauze of cotton	40	1/93–12/94
6116	Gloves and mittens of cotton	60/40	1/93–12/94
6302	Toilet linen and kitchen linen of cotton	75/50	1/93–12/94
6601	Umbrellas and parasols	72	1/93–12/94
6603	Parts and accessories of umbrellas	72	1/93–12/94
6814	Articles of mica	30	1/93–12/93
6902	Refractory bricks	51	1/93–12/93
7003	Cast glass and rolled glass (2–3 mm in thickness)	40	1/93–12/94
7004	Drawn glass and blown glass (2–6 mm in thickness)	40	1/93–12/94
7005	Float glass and surface ground glass (2–3 mm, 4–6 mm)	40	1/93–12/94
7107	Base metals clad with silver (plates, sheets, strips)	11/8	1/93–12/94

Appendix Table A.2 (continued)

Code of Korea	Description	Tariff rate[a] (percent)	Period
7109	Base metals or silver, clad with gold (plates, sheets, trips)	11/8	1/93–12/94
7315	Iron or steel chains	20	1/93–12/94
7606	Aluminum plates and sheets	20	1/93–12/94
8204	Hand-operated spanners	22	1/93–12/93
8413	Pumps for liquids	20	1/93–12/94
8425	Pulley tackle and hoists (of a freight-lifting capacity not exceeding 10 million tons)	20	1/93–12/94
8471	Computer motherboards	25/20	1/93–12/94
8473	Computer motherboards	20/15	1/93–12/94
8482	Ball bearings	30	1/93–12/94
8506	Primary cells and batteries (manganese, alkali manganese)	30	1/93–12/94
8533	Electrical resistors (fixed resistors)	18	1/93–12/94
	Electrical resistors (varisters)	50	1/93–12/94
9001	Plastic vision correction lenses	30	1/93–12/94
9003	Plastic or precious metal eyeglass frames	30	1/93–12/04

a. Numbers after slashes correspond to the tariff rates applied in 1994.

Source: Korean Ministry of Finance.

Appendix Table A.3 Items under flexible tariff system: antidumping duties

HS Code of Korea	Description (country of origin)	Tariff rate (percent)	Period
3907.10.0000	Polyacetals (US, Japan)	4 - (by setting base import prices)	9/91–8/93
2809.20.1000	Phosphoric acid (China)	44.73–59.34	10/92–1/93
		40.96–54.28	2/93–1/96
8482.10.0000	Ball bearings for head drum of VTR	12.5	10/92–1/93
	(Thailand)	6.27	1/93–12/97
3701.30.9100	Photographic plates for graphic	28.70	11/93–10/98
91.9100	art (Japan)	38.18	
99.9100		24.51	
2836.20.0000	Sodium ash (China)	66.11	1/94–12/96
7019.10.0000	Glass fibers (US, Japan, Taiwan)	10.3–58.7	4/94–3/99
31.0000			

Source: Korean Ministry of Finance.

Appendix Table A.4 Items under flexible tariff system: tariff quotas

HS Code of Korea	Description	Tariff rates[a] (percent)	Quota (for lower tariff)	Period
1507	Soybean oil	13-9/25	15,000 metric tons	6/91–6/93
		9-8/20	20,000 metric tons	6/93–6/94
0803	Bananas	40/90	50,000 metric tons	1/92–12/93
		30/90	30,000 metric tons	12/93–6/94
7501	Nickel oxide[b]	5	Total amount	1/94–6/94

a. Numbers before the slashes represent in-quota tariff rates that were basic (statutory) rates. Basic rates were lowered in steps under the 5-year Tariff Reduction Plan (1989–94); thus, soybean oil has two numbers before the slash that represent an upper and lower range of the in-quota tariff rates in this period. Numbers after the slashes represent beyond-quota tariff rates, which were higher than basic rates.
b. The statutory tariff rate for nickel oxide was 2 percent. However, since the quota was set to the total amount imported during the period, the applied tariff rate was 5 percent.

Source: Korean Ministry of Finance.

Appendix Table A.5 Items under flexible tariff system: emergency tariffs

HS Code of Korea	Description	Tariff rate (percent)	Period
2526	Natural steatite	30	7/91–6/93
1602	Pork in airtight containers	40	7/91–6/93
3902.10	Polyethylene film	25	10/90–9/92

Source: Korean Ministry of Finance.

Appendix Table A.6 Import restrictions of agricultural items under consolidated public notice

Underlying laws	Major items	Number of items
Foodgrain Control Act, A :mal Feed Management Act, and Major Agricultural Seed Act	Rice, barley, soybeans, green beans, beer barley, buckwheat, oats, millet, Indian millet, sweet potatoes, potatoes, corn, starches, peanuts, residues of sesame oil extractions, powdered bones, animal fodder	71
Seedling Management Act	Apple, pear, peach, and orange trees, vegetable seeds	5
Sericulture Act	Silkworm eggs, mulberry trees	2
Livestock Act	Purebred breeding cows, swine and chickens, bird eggs, animal semen and embryos	10
Ginseng Business Act	Ginseng and its products	18
Tobacco Business Act	Leaf tobacco and its products	12
Fisheries Act	Live fishes, crustaceans, mollusks, aquatic invertebrates, laver, other seaweed	12
Total		130

Source: Korea Rural Economic Institute 1991.

Appendix Table A.7　Import restrictions of agricultural items under export-import public notice

Sectors	Major items	Number of items
Agriculture		
Cereals	Malt	3
Potatoes	Manioc (cassava)	3
Vegetables	Peppers, garlic, ginger, and other vegetables	12
Fruits and nuts	Citrus fruits, apples, grapes, peaches, sweet persimmons, and their juices and products	27
Edible oil	Sesame oil, peanut oil and preparations, other nonvolatile vegetable oils	3
Sugars	Molasses, sucrose	4
Teas	Green tea, black tea	4
Alcohol	Fermented beverages from cereals (cheong ju, takju, etc.)	8
Others	Hof cones, bean curd, vegetable protein concentrates, other vegetable products	5
Livestock and product		
Livestock	Deer	6
Meat	Meat and its preparations (of bovine animals, swine, poultry)	35
Dairy products	Milk, milk powder, condensed milk, butter, cheese, whey, curd	31
Others	Natural honey and its preparations, artificial honey, egg yolks, edible flours, and meals of meat	6
Forestry		
Nuts	Chestnuts, pine nuts, jujubes, other nuts	7
Fisheries		
Fish	Shark, sardines, mackerel, Alaska pollack, horse mackerel, tuna, yellow corvina, anchovies	54
Fish preparations	Fish cake, tuna preparations	11
Crustaceans	Crabs, shrimp, peeled shrimp and its preparations	7
Mollusks	Squid and its preparations, octopus, abalone, cockles	20
Aquatic animals	Sea squirts, sea cucumbers	3
Seaweed	Laver	3
Others	Whale meat, fish fillets, fish egg	12
Total		273

Source: Korea Rural Economic Institute 1991.

Appendix Table A.8　Concordance between the HS Code of Korea (HSK) and the Korean SIC (KSIC)

Products/Sectors	HS	KSIC (Product classification in *SYAFF*)[a]
Beef	0202	01212
Pork	0203	01221
Poultry	0207	01222, 01223
Ivory, antlers, etc.	0507	01229* (Young antlers)
Dried onions and garlic	0712	15139102
Dried beans	0713	01111* (Red beans, green beans, kidney beans)
Nuts	0802	01131* (Chestnut, walnut, pine nut, ginkgo nut)
Bananas	0803	01131* (Banana)
Peppers	0904	01121* (Red peppers)
Barley	1003	01111* (Barley, naked barley, beer barley)
Corn	1005	01111* (Corn)
Milled rice	1006	01111* (Rice)
Malt	1107	155311
Soybeans	1201	01111* (Soybeans)
Peanuts	1202	01111* (Peanuts)
Oilseeds	1207	01119* (Sesame, perilla seed, rape)
Fish	0301-2	051*, 0521* (Fish)
Crabs, lobster, and shrimp	0306	051*, 0521* (Crustacea)
Dairy products	0401-6	01211
Vegetable extracts	1302	02013* (Korean laogner), 15495103, 15495104, 15495106, 15495109
Prepared meat and fish	16	15119, 1512 (not 15121)
Other sugars	1702	15209101, 153221, 15459102
Pasta	1902	154401, 154402
Prepared fruits and vegetables	20	1513, 154304
Tea and roasted coffee	2101	15491, 15492
Sauces and prepared sauces	2103	15451, 154521, 154523, 15453, 15454
Other food preparations	2106	154591 (not 15459102), 15494, 15495105, 15496, 15498
Distilled liquor	2208	1551
Leaf tobacco	2401	16001
Natural steatite	2526	14210307
Cosmetics	3304	24245102, 24245109, 242452, 24245402, 24245403
Toilet preparations	3307	24245404, 24245405, 24249103
Casein	3501	24293101
Plywood	4412	202121
Wooden tableware and kitchenware	4419	202951
Carpets	57	1722
Knitted apparel	61	173 (not 17301)
Other apparel	62	181 (not 18127)
Other textile articles	63	17211, 17212, 17213, 17214, 17215
Porcelain household articles	6911	269121
Glassware	7013	261061
Glass beads and imitation pearls	7018	26109101, 26109102, 26109103
Stoves and ranges	7321	293063
Steel household articles	7323	289132, 28932 (not 28932109), 28992, 289931
Aluminum household articles	7615	289131, 28993201
Sound reproduction apparatus	8519	32300206, 323003

Appendix Table A.8 (continued)

Products/sectors	HS	KSIC (Product classification in SYAFF)[a]
Video reproduction apparatus	8521	32300112, 33204108, 33204111, 33204112
Motor vehicles for people	8703	341021
Motor vehicles for goods	8704	34102301, 34102302, 34102303, 34102304, 34102305, 34102306
Electric musical instruments	9207	369261
Equipment for games	9504	369441, 369491
Sporting goods	9506	369311, 369321, 369391

a. *Statistical Yearbook of Agriculture, Forestry, and Fisheries (SYAFF).*

Note: The asterisk (*) means that the product range of the corresponding HS code is a subset of the category defined by the KSIC code. The item names in parentheses following asterisks are the subproduct ranges in the KSIC code that match most closely with the range of the HS code. Those subproduct ranges are defined in the *SYAFF* on the basis of the KSIC code.

Sources: Korean National Statistical Office 1991; Korean Ministry of Agriculture, Forestry and Fisheries 1993.

Appendix Table A.9   Elasticities estimated in other studies

Items (sources)	Demand elasticities of domestic goods (Edd/Edm)	Demand elasticities of imported goods (Emm/Emd)	Supply elasticities of domestic goods[a]
Meat (J-SUK)	−0.21	−0.95	0.38
Beef (KREI)	−0.97		1.25 (−2)
Pork (KREI)	−0.43		0.48 (−2)
Chicken (KREI)	−0.60		0.36 (−2)
Milled rice (KREI)	−0.29		0.78 (−1)
Milled rice (J-SUK)	−0.10	−0.94	0.05
Wheat (J-SUK)	−0.20	−0.27	0.50
Barley (KREI)	−0.26		0.31 (−1)
Beer barley (KREI)	−2.83		0.12 (−1)
Soybeans (J-SUK)	−0.18	−0.20	0.50
Potatoes (KREI)	−0.47		0.45 (−1)
Garlic (KREI)	−0.30		0.38
Onions (KREI)	−0.68		0.39
Peppers (KREI)	−0.22		0.36
Oranges (KREI)	−0.62		
Citrus fruits (J-SUK)	−0.15	−0.30	0.35
Tobacco products (J-SUK)	−0.52	−1.89	0.55
Peanuts (US-HE)	−0.73/0.10	−13.00/13.00	1.60
Sugars (US-HE)	−1.33/1.30	−3.78/3.69	0.60
Dairy products (J-SUK)	−0.10	−0.33	1.60
Dairy products (US-HE)	−0.37/0.10	−1.66/1.34	0.60
Canned tuna (US-HE)	−1.18/0.68	−2.33/1.84	1.00
Processed meat products (J-SUK)	−0.17	−0.73	0.72
Canned or bottled vegetables and fruits (J-SUK)	−1.09	−2.26	0.50
Frozen concentrated orange juice (US-HE)	−1.05/0.55	−1.85/1.35	1.00
Bread (J-SUK)	−0.13	−0.87	0.27
Beer (J-SUK)	−0.16	−0.80	0.99
Whiskey and brandy (J-SUK)	−0.40	−0.69	0.50
Cosmetics, toilet preparations (J-SUK)	−0.14	−0.47	1.74
Benzenoid chemicals (US-HE)	−0.20/0.20	−1.42/1.42	1.80
Polyethylene resins (US-HE)	−0.90/0.33	−5.09/4.50	2.00
Softwood lumber (US-HE)	−1.45/0.85	−3.15/2.55	0.32
Plywood (J-SUK)	−0.13	−1.24	0.50
Knit fabrics (J-SUK)	−0.30	−1.75	0.26
Clothing (J-SUK)	−0.12	−0.64	0.73
Textiles (US-HE)	−1.40/1.18	−1.60/1.10	1.00
Apparel (US-HE)	−0.60/0.21	−1.30/1.30	1.00
Sheet glass (J-SUK)	−1.06	−1.50	0.50
Ceramic articles (US-HE)	−2.27/2.27	−1.03/1.00	2.00
Ceramic tiles (US-HE)	−0.44/0.44	−0.50/0.50	0.60
Glassware (US-HE)	−0.70/0.70	−2.86/2.86	1.00
Costume jewelry (US-HE)	−1.65/1.65	−3.77/3.77	2.45
Steel products (US-HE)	−1.08/0.52	−3.25/2.69	0.65
Ball bearings (US-HE)	−0.10/0.10	−0.28/0.28	1.00
Machine tools (US-HE)	−0.73/0.69	−0.79/0.79	1.00
Radio and TV sets (J-SUK)	−0.27	−1.97	0.55
Communication equipment (J-SUK)	−0.11	−1.24	1.21

Appendix Table A.9   (continued)

Items (sources)	Demand elasticities of domestic goods (*Edd/Edm*)	Demand elasticities of imported goods (*Emm/Emd*)	Supply elasticities of domestic goods[a]
Semiconductors (US-HE)	− 1.80/1.47	− 1.70/1.06	2.00
Automobiles (US-HE)	− 1.19/0.30	− 1.50/0.60	1.00
Minivans (US-HE)	− 1.19/0.10	− 1.50/1.50	1.00
Leather footwear (J-SUK)	− 0.28	− 2.69	1.88
Women's handbags (US-HE)	− 4.44/1.93	− 2.01/1.40	2.00
Women's footwear (US-HE)	− 4.90/4.90	− 2.00/2.00	3.00
Rubber footwear (US-HE)	− 2.83/2.83	− 2.00/2.00	2.00
Luggage (US-HE)	− 2.06/0.41	− 1.82/0.53	2.00

a. The numbers in parentheses indicate time lags. For example, 0.48 (− 2) for pork means that the supply elasticity for pork prices from two years ago is 0.48.

Sources: Korea Rural Economic Institute 1993 (KREI); Hufbauer and Elliott 1994 (US-HE). Sazanami, Urata, and Kawai 1995 (J-SUK).

Appendix B

Appendix Table B.1   Base-year data by product category, 1992

Product category	Imports (billions of 1992 won)	Domestic production (billions of 1992 won)	Employment (thousands of workers)[a]	Collected tariff rate[b]	Tariff equivalent of calculated tariff plus nontariff barriers[c]
Beef	375.0	1,601	207.1	0.20	1.69
Pork	2.0	1,251	161.8	0.21	0.51
Poultry	29.0	506	65.4	0.20	0.65
Ivory, antlers, etc.	44.0	9	1.2	0.25	n.a.
Dried onions and garlic	29.0	40	5.2	0.53	2.60
Dried beans	11.9	60	7.8	0.30	4.94
Nuts	19.7	120	14.5	0.35	2.33
Bananas	63.2	3	0.4	0.85	n.a.
Peppers	11.0	1,041	134.7	0.39	3.00
Barley	9.7	293	37.9	0.35	4.24
Corn	664.5	24	3.1	0.03	3.65
Milled rice	0.4	6,723	869.6	0.05	5.95
Malt	17.3	115	14.9	0.35	2.99
Soybeans	259.2	199	25.8	0.03	5.41
Peanuts	8.8	51	6.6	0.40	2.60
Oilseeds	24.8	303	39.2	0.35	4.93
Fish	12.0	1,272	48.4	0.47	n.a.
Crab, lobster, and shrimp	17.6	219	8.3	0.18	n.a.
Dairy products	26.5	1,861	11.5	0.22	1.50
Vegetable extracts	34.1	86	1.1	0.13	n.a.
Prepared meat and fish	30.7	2,179	39.8	0.25	n.a.
Other sugars	10.2	184	1.5	0.18	n.a.
Pasta	15.9	778	10.8	0.45	n.a.
Prepared fruits and vegetables	167.7	641	11.4	0.43	n.a.
Tea and roasted coffee	14.6	433	2.5	0.18	n.a.
Sauces and prepared sauces	18.6	813	7.6	0.14	n.a.
Other food preparations	65.7	739	23.7	0.13	n.a.
Distilled liquor	38.5	847	4.3	0.40	n.a.
Leaf tobacco	53.5	326	1.7	0.20	0.71
Natural steatite	12.1	23	0.4	0.12	n.a.
Cosmetics	33.6	584	5.8	0.13	n.a.
Toilet preparations	10.5	21	0.2	0.13	n.a.
Casein	25.6	289	3.2	0.20	n.a.
Plywood	274.5	509	6.7	0.15	n.a.
Wooden tableware and kitchenware	8.0	22	1.2	0.47	n.a.
Carpets	21.6	59	1.3	0.13	n.a.
Apparel	192.2	7,276	225.4	0.13	n.a.
Other textile articles	30.0	956	23.7	0.16	n.a.
Porcelain household articles	11.8	188	9.2	0.13	n.a.
Glassware	27.4	69	2.1	0.13	n.a.
Glass beads and imitation pearls	22.0	31	0.3	0.13	n.a.
Stoves and ranges	20.7	385	3.9	0.13	n.a.
Steel household articles	15.5	692	17.2	0.13	n.a.
Aluminum household articles	8.7	132	3.2	0.13	n.a.
Motor vehicles for people	45.3	7,735	46.7	0.16	n.a.
Motor vehicles for goods	84.9	2,606	15.7	0.17	n.a.
Electric musical instruments	9.5	113	0.6	0.13	n.a.
Equipment for games	114.7	68	1.0	0.13	n.a.
Sporting goods	59.7	199	5.0	0.14	n.a.

a. In the agricultural sector, the employment figures for individual products are calculated as the total number of agricultural employees multiplied by the production weight (in value terms) of each product. Most Korean farmers concurrently raise several different crops and livestock, so it is impossible to speak of workers "dedicated" to a particular commodity.
b. The calculated tariff rate is measured as the realized tariff revenue collected divided by the total value of imports on a c.i.f. basis, using the average exchange rate for 1992 ($1 = 780$ won).
c. The tariff equivalent of nontariff barriers was not estimated for the products indicated by "n.a."

Sources: Korean Customs Service and Korea Customs Research Institute 1993; Korean National Statistical Office 1994; Korean Ministry of Agriculture, Forestry, and Fisheries 1993; Economic Planning Board 1992; Uruguay Round Schedule LX 1994.

Appendix Table B.2 Parameters used in the partial computable equilibrium model

Product category	Parameter[a]	Demand elasticity				Domestic supply elasticity (Es)
		Edd	Edm	Emm	Emd	
Beef	Group A	−0.20	0.14	−0.71	0.50	0.20
	Group B	−0.50	0.35	−0.78	1.25	0.30
Pork	Group A	−0.20	0.14	−9.43	6.60	0.20
	Group B	−0.50	0.35	−12.20	8.54	0.50
Poultry	Group A	−0.20	0.14	−2.91	2.03	0.20
	Group B	−0.50	0.35	−7.27	5.09	0.50
Ivory, antlers, etc.	Group A	−1.22	0.85	−0.20	0.14	0.20
	Group B	−3.05	2.14	−0.50	0.35	0.50
Dried onions and garlic	Group A	−0.22	0.16	−0.20	0.14	0.20
	Group B	−0.56	0.39	−0.50	0.35	0.50
Dried beans	Group A	−0.20	0.14	−0.77	0.54	0.20
	Group B	−0.50	0.35	−1.93	1.35	0.50
Nuts	Group A	−0.20	0.14	−0.89	0.62	0.20
	Group B	−0.50	0.35	−2.23	1.56	0.50
Bananas	Group A	−3.00	2.10	−0.20	0.14	0.20
	Group B	−7.50	5.25	−0.50	0.35	0.50
Peppers	Group A	−0.20	0.14	−2.18	1.53	0.20
	Group B	−0.50	0.35	−2.93	2.05	0.50
Barley	Group A	−0.20	0.14	−1.17	0.82	0.20
	Group B	−0.50	0.35	−1.73	1.21	0.50
Corn	Group A	−3.00	2.10	−0.20	0.14	0.20
	Group B	−7.50	5.25	−0.50	0.35	0.50
Milled rice	Group A	−0.20	0.14	−5.24	3.67	0.20
	Group B	−0.50	0.35	−5.80	4.06	0.50
Malt	Group A	−0.20	0.14	−1.00	0.70	0.20
	Group B	−0.50	0.35	−2.51	1.76	0.50
Soybeans	Group A	−0.27	0.19	−0.20	0.14	0.20
	Group B	−0.67	0.47	−0.50	0.35	0.50
Peanuts	Group A	−0.20	0.14	−0.81	0.57	0.20
	Group B	−0.50	0.35	−2.02	1.41	0.50
Oilseeds	Group A	−0.20	0.14	−0.67	0.47	0.20
	Group B	−0.50	0.35	−1.09	0.76	0.50
Fish	Group A	−0.20	0.14	−4.61	3.23	0.20
	Group B	−0.50	0.35	−7.10	4.97	0.50
Crab, lobster, and shrimp	Group A	−0.20	0.14	−2.07	1.45	0.20
	Group B	−0.50	0.35	−5.17	3.62	0.50
Dairy products	Group A	−0.30	0.21	−2.91	2.04	0.30
	Group B	−0.75	0.53	−4.01	2.81	0.75
Vegetable extracts	Group A	−0.30	0.21	−0.67	0.47	0.30
	Group B	−0.75	0.53	−1.68	1.18	0.75
Prepared meat and fish	Group A	−0.30	0.21	−5.75	4.03	0.30
	Group B	−0.75	0.53	−11.25	7.88	0.75
Other sugars	Group A	−0.30	0.21	−4.50	3.15	0.30
	Group B	−0.75	0.53	−11.25	7.88	0.75
Pasta	Group A	−0.30	0.21	−4.50	3.15	0.30
	Group B	−0.75	0.53	−11.25	7.88	0.75
Prepared fruits and vegetables	Group A	−0.30	0.21	−0.80	0.56	0.30
	Group B	−0.75	0.53	−2.00	1.40	0.75
Tea and roasted coffee	Group A	−0.30	0.21	−4.50	3.15	0.30
	Group B	−0.75	0.53	−11.25	7.88	0.75

Appendix Table B.2 (continued)

Product category	Parameters	Demand elasticities Edd	Edm	Emm	Emd	Domestic supply elasticity (Es)
Sauces and prepared sauces	Group A	−0.30	0.21	−4.50	3.15	0.30
	Group B	−0.75	0.53	−11.25	7.88	0.75
Other food preparations	Group A	−0.30	0.21	−2.97	2.08	0.30
	Group B	−0.75	0.53	−7.43	5.20	0.75
Distilled liquor	Group A	−0.30	0.21	−4.50	3.15	0.30
	Group B	−0.75	0.53	−11.25	7.88	0.75
Leaf tobacco	Group A	−0.30	0.21	−1.54	1.08	0.30
	Group B	−0.75	0.53	−3.85	2.70	0.75
Natural steatite	Group A	−0.40	0.28	−0.68	0.48	0.40
	Group B	−1.00	0.70	−1.71	1.19	1.00
Cosmetics	Group A	−0.40	0.28	−6.00	4.20	0.40
	Group B	−1.00	0.70	−15.00	10.50	1.00
Toilet preparations	Group A	−0.40	0.28	−0.74	0.52	0.40
	Group B	−1.00	0.70	−1.86	1.30	1.00
Casein	Group A	−0.40	0.28	−3.70	2.59	0.40
	Group B	−1.00	0.70	−9.26	6.48	1.00
Plywood	Group A	−0.50	0.35	−0.81	0.56	0.50
	Group B	−1.50	1.05	−2.42	1.69	1.50
Wooden tableware and kitchenware	Group A	−0.50	0.35	−0.94	0.66	0.50
	Group B	−1.50	1.05	−2.81	1.97	1.50
Carpets	Group A	−0.50	0.35	−1.19	0.83	0.50
	Group B	−1.50	1.05	−3.56	2.49	1.50
Apparel	Group A	−0.50	0.35	−7.50	5.25	0.50
	Group B	−1.50	1.05	−22.50	15.75	1.50
Other textile articles	Group A	−0.50	0.35	−7.50	5.25	0.50
	Group B	−1.50	1.05	−22.50	15.75	1.50
Porcelain household articles	Group A	−0.50	0.35	−6.93	4.85	0.50
	Group B	−1.50	1.05	−20.78	14.55	1.50
Glassware	Group A	−0.50	0.35	−1.13	0.79	0.50
	Group B	−1.50	1.05	−3.39	2.37	1.50
Glass beads and imitation pearls	Group A	−0.50	0.35	−0.62	0.44	0.50
	Group B	−1.50	1.05	−1.87	1.31	1.50
Stoves and ranges	Group A	−0.50	0.35	−7.50	5.25	0.50
	Group B	−1.25	0.88	−18.75	13.13	1.25
Steel household articles	Group A	−0.50	0.35	−7.50	5.25	0.50
	Group B	−1.25	0.88	−18.75	13.13	1.25
Aluminum household articles	Group A	−0.50	0.35	−6.49	4.54	0.50
	Group B	−1.25	0.88	−16.23	11.36	1.25
Motor vehicles for people	Group A	−0.50	0.35	−14.88	10.42	0.50
	Group B	−1.25	0.88	−21.74	15.22	1.25
Motor vehicles for goods	Group A	−0.50	0.35	−7.50	5.25	0.50
	Group B	−1.25	0.88	−18.75	13.13	1.25
Electric musical instruments	Group A	−0.50	0.35	−5.58	3.91	0.50
	Group B	−2.00	1.40	−22.32	15.62	2.00
Equipment for games	Group A	−0.96	0.67	−0.50	0.35	0.50
	Group B	−3.84	2.69	−2.00	1.40	2.00
Sporting goods	Group A	−0.50	0.35	−1.46	1.02	0.50
	Group B	−2.00	1.40	−5.84	4.09	2.00

Edd = own-price elasticity of demand for domestic goods; Edm = cross-price elasticity of demand for domestic goods with respect to imported goods; Emm = own-price elasticity of demand for imported goods; Emd = cross-price elasticity of demand for imported goods with respect to domestic goods; Es = own-price elasticity of supply for domestic producers.

a. Group A represents a "bundle" of low elasticity values; Group B represents a "bundle" of high elasticity values.

Appendix Table B.3 Calculated effects of removing protection on imports, domestic production, and employment, 1992[a]

Product category	Parameter	Import price (index)[b]	Import quantity (billions of 1992 won)	Change in import quantity (percent)	Domestic price (index)[c]	Domestic production quantity (billions of 1992 won)	Change in domestic production quantity (percent)	Employment (thousands of workers)	Change in Employment (percent)[d]
Beef	Group A	0.37	637.4	70	0.71	1,493.9	−7	193.2	−7
	Group B	0.37	1,412.4	277	0.71	1,346.4	−16	174.2	−16
Pork	Group A	0.66	37.6	1,780	0.87	1,215.4	−3	157.2	−3
	Group B	0.66	89.0	4,352	0.87	1,164.0	−7	150.5	−7
Poultry	Group A	0.61	87.0	200	0.84	488.6	−3	63.2	−3
	Group B	0.61	452.2	1,459	0.84	463.5	−8	59.9	−8
Ivory, antlers, etc.	Group A	0.80	45.1	3	0.88	8.8	−3	1.2	−3
	Group B	0.80	46.9	7	0.88	8.4	−6	1.1	−7
Dried onions and garlic	Group A	0.28	35.1	21	0.63	36.4	−9	4.7	−9
	Group B	0.28	46.6	61	0.62	31.6	−21	4.1	−21
Dried beans	Group A	0.17	33.5	182	0.54	53.0	−12	6.9	−12
	Group B	0.17	158.5	1,232	0.54	43.9	−27	5.7	−27
Nuts	Group A	0.30	44.3	125	0.66	110.3	−8	13.3	−8
	Group B	0.30	149.3	658	0.66	97.2	−19	11.8	−19
Bananas	Group A	0.54	67.6	7	0.67	2.8	−8	0.4	−8
	Group B	0.54	74.6	18	0.67	2.5	−18	0.3	−18
Peppers	Group A	0.25	107.7	879	0.62	944.7	−9	122.2	−9
	Group B	0.25	236.2	2,047	0.62	816.8	−22	105.7	−22
Barley	Group A	0.19	41.9	332	0.56	260.9	−11	33.8	−11
	Group B	0.19	84.5	771	0.56	219.2	−25	28.4	−25
Corn	Group A	0.22	784.6	18	0.36	19.6	−18	2.5	−18
	Group B	0.22	1,006.7	52	0.36	14.5	−40	1.9	−40
Milled rice	Group A	0.14	857.3	214,219	0.51	5,869.8	−13	759.2	−13
	Group B	0.14	1,945.9	486,365	0.51	4,788.7	−29	619.4	−29

Product	Group								
Malt	Group A	0.25	49.3	185	0.62	104.4	−9	13.5	−9
	Group B	0.25	237.0	1,270	0.62	90.3	−22	11.7	−22
Soybeans	Group A	0.16	338.5	31	0.47	171.4	−14	22.2	−14
	Group B	0.16	505.7	95	0.47	137.1	−31	17.8	−31
Peanuts	Group A	0.28	19.1	117	0.64	46.7	−9	6.0	−9
	Group B	0.28	61.1	594	0.64	40.8	−20	5.3	−20
Oilseeds	Group A	0.17	61.0	146	0.54	267.5	−12	34.6	−12
	Group B	0.17	107.3	333	0.54	221.9	−27	28.7	−27
Fish	Group A	0.68	46.1	284	0.87	1,238.0	−3	47.1	−3
	Group B	0.68	95.3	694	0.87	1,188.8	−7	45.2	−7
Crab, lobster, and shrimp	Group A	0.85	22.7	29	0.94	216.5	−1	8.2	−1
	Group B	0.85	33.3	89	0.94	212.8	−3	8.1	−3
Dairy products	Group A	0.40	198.6	649	0.73	1,690.2	−9	10.4	−9
	Group B	0.40	425.2	1,504	0.73	1,463.0	−21	9.0	−21
Vegetable extracts	Group A	0.89	36.3	6	0.96	84.9	−1	1.1	−1
	Group B	0.89	39.8	17	0.96	83.3	−3	1.1	−3
Prepared meat and fish	Group A	0.80	81.7	166	0.92	2,128.0	−2	38.9	−2
	Group B	0.80	208.5	579	0.92	2,053.7	−6	37.5	−6
Other sugars	Group A	0.85	17.7	73	0.94	180.9	−2	1.5	−2
	Group B	0.85	40.4	296	0.94	176.3	−4	1.4	−4
Pasta	Group A	0.69	55.7	250	0.88	748.5	−4	10.4	−4
	Group B	0.69	364.6	2,193	0.88	706.2	−9	9.8	−9
Prepared fruits and vegetables	Group A	0.70	208.3	24	0.38	617.3	−4	11.0	−4
	Group B	0.70	288.3	72	0.88	583.5	−9	10.4	−9
Tea and roasted coffee	Group A	0.85	25.3	73	0.94	425.7	−2	2.5	−2
	Group B	0.85	57.9	296	0.94	415.0	−4	2.4	−4
Sauces and prepared sauces	Group A	0.88	28.7	54	0.56	802.2	−1	7.5	−1
	Group B	0.88	54.9	195	0.56	786.2	−3	7.4	−3
Other food preparations	Group A	0.88	86.6	32	0.96	729.5	−1	23.4	−1
	Group B	0.88	131.0	99	0.95	715.5	−3	23.0	−3
Distilled liquor	Group A	0.72	119.3	210	0.89	817.9	−3	4.2	−3
	Group B	0.72	650.8	1590	0.89	776.1	−8	3.9	−8

continued next page

Appendix Table B.3 (continued)

Product category	Parameters	Import price (index)[b]	Import quantity (billions of 1992 won)	Change in import quantity (percent)	Domestic price (index)[c]	Domestic production quantity (billions of 1992 won)	Change in domestic production quantity (percent)	Employment (thousands of workers)	Change in Employment (percent)[d]
Leaf tobacco	Group A	0.58	99.8	87	0.83	308.1	−5	1.6	−5
	Group B	0.58	254.2	375	0.83	282.2	−13	1.5	−13
Natural steatite	Group A	0.89	12.9	6	0.96	22.6	−2	0.4	−3
	Group B	0.89	14.1	16	0.96	22.1	−4	0.4	−5
Cosmetics	Group A	0.88	58.7	75	0.96	574.0	−2	5.7	−2
	Group B	0.88	135.5	303	0.96	559.4	−4	5.6	−4
Toilet preparations	Group A	0.88	11.3	7	0.96	20.6	−2	0.2	−2
	Group B	0.88	12.5	19	0.96	20.1	−4	0.2	−5
Casein	Group A	0.83	42.7	67	0.94	281.7	−3	3.1	−3
	Group B	0.83	92.1	260	0.94	271.1	−6	3.0	−6
Plywood	Group A	0.87	298.8	9	0.95	496.7	−2	6.5	−2
	Group B	0.87	354.2	29	0.95	473.0	−7	6.2	−7
Wooden tableware and kitchenware	Group A	0.68	10.5	31	0.87	20.6	−6	1.1	−7
	Group B	0.68	18.1	126	0.87	18.0	−18	1.0	−18
Carpets	Group A	0.88	24.1	12	0.96	57.8	−2	1.3	−2
	Group B	0.88	30.0	39	0.96	55.3	−6	1.2	−6
Apparel	Group A	0.88	391.7	104	0.96	7,117.6	−2	220.5	−2
	Group B	0.88	1,627.4	747	0.96	6,811.2	−6	211.0	−6
Other textile articles	Group A	0.86	70.9	136	0.95	930.9	−3	23.1	−3
	Group B	0.86	395.8	1,219	0.95	882.7	−8	21.9	−8
Porcelain household articles	Group A	0.88	22.5	90	0.96	184.0	−2	9.0	−2
	Group B	0.88	81.4	590	0.96	176.2	−6	8.6	−6
Glassware	Group A	0.88	30.4	11	0.96	67.5	−2	2.1	−2
	Group B	0.88	37.6	37	0.96	64.7	−6	2.0	−6

Glass beads and imitation pearls	Group A	0.88	23.3	6	0.96	30.3	−2	0.3	−3
	Group B	0.88	26.2	19	0.96	29.1	−6	0.3	−7
Stoves and ranges	Group A	0.88	41.6	101	0.96	376.8	−2	3.8	−2
	Group B	0.88	118.3	471	0.96	364.8	−5	3.7	−5
Steel household articles	Group A	0.89	30.5	97	0.96	677.7	−2	16.8	−2
	Group B	0.89	84.2	443	0.96	656.7	−5	16.3	−5
Aluminum household articles	Group A	0.88	15.8	82	0.96	129.2	−2	3.1	−2
	Group B	0.88	38.9	347	0.96	125.1	−5	3.0	−5
Motor vehicles for people	Group A	0.86	247.1	445	0.95	7,533.3	−3	45.5	−3
	Group B	0.86	540.1	1,092	0.95	7,240.5	−6	43.7	−6
Motor vehicles for goods	Group A	0.85	206.5	143	0.95	2,535.4	−3	15.3	−3
	Group B	0.85	783.7	823	0.95	2,433.0	−7	14.7	−7
Electric musical instruments	Group A	0.89	15.6	64	0.96	110.7	−2	0.6	−2
	Group B	0.89	69.1	628	0.96	104.1	−8	0.6	−8
Equipment for games	Group A	0.88	119.6	4	0.94	66.1	−3	1.0	−3
	Group B	0.88	135.5	18	0.94	60.7	−11	0.9	−11
Sporting goods	Group A	0.88	68.8	15	0.96	194.6	−2	4.9	−2
	Group B	0.88	105.2	76	0.96	181.9	−9	4.6	−9

a. Figures for sectors and totals are value-weighted averages of subdivided items, using import values or domestic production values, as appropriate.
b. The import price index indicates the landed price of imports, after total liberalization, relative to the price before liberalization (index value of 1.00).
c. The domestic price index indicates the price of domestic goods, after total liberalization, relative to the price before liberalization (index value of 1.00).
d. The percentage change in employment is assumed to be the same as the percentage change in domestic production.

Source: Author's estimates.

Appendix Table B.4 Calculated welfare effects of removing protection, 1992
(billions of 1992 won unless noted otherwise)

Product category	Parameter	Consumer surplus gain (A+B+C+D)	Producer surplus loss (A)	Tariff revenue decline (B)	Quota rents eliminated[a] (C)	Efficiency gain (D)	Consumer surplus cost per job[b] (million won)	Efficiency cost per job[c] (million won)
Beef	Group A	771	453	63	173	82	56	6
	Group B	993	431	63	173	326	30	10
Pork	Group A	172	166	0	1	6	37	1
	Group B	178	162	1	0	15	16	1
Poultry	Group A	103	80	5	7	11	46	5
	Group B	173	78	5	7	83	31	15
Ivory, antlers, etc.	Group A	10	1	9	n.a.	0	316	2
	Group B	10	1	9	n.a.	0	131	2
Dried onions and garlic	Group A	37	14	10	11	2	80	5
	Group B	40	13	10	11	6	37	6
Dried beans	Group A	45	26	3	7	9	49	10
	Group B	95	24	3	7	61	45	29
Nuts	Group A	63	40	5	9	9	53	7
	Group B	96	37	5	9	45	35	16
Bananas	Group A	31	1	29	n.a.	1	992	32
	Group B	33	1	29	n.a.	3	445	36
Peppers	Group A	426	382	3	5	36	34	3
	Group B	449	357	3	5	84	16	3
Barley	Group A	143	122	3	5	13	34	3
	Group B	151	113	3	5	30	16	3
Corn	Group A	583	14	17	505	47	1,029	83
	Group B	668	12	17	505	134	544	109
Milled rice	Group A	3,469	3,102	0	0	367	31	3
	Group B	3,669	2,836	0	0	833	15	3

Malt	Group A	66	42	4	8	12	49	9
	Group B	133	39	4	8	82	42	26
Soybeans	Group A	350	97	8	211	34	98	9
	Group B	411	88	8	211	104	51	13
Peanuts	Group A	29	18	3	4	4	49	7
	Group B	42	16	3	4	19	32	14
Oilseeds	Group A	167	132	6	14	15	37	3
	Group B	176	122	6	14	34	17	3
Fish	Group A	168	159	4	n.a.	5	130	4
	Group B	173	156	4	n.a.	13	55	4
Crab, lobster, and shrimp	Group A	15	12	3	n.a.	0	160	4
	Group B	16	12	3	n.a.	1	68	5
Dairy products	Group A	555	487	5	11	52	526	49
	Group B	592	456	5	11	120	241	49
Vegetable extracts	Group A	8	4	4	n.a.	0	598	10
	Group B	8	4	4	n.a.	0	224	9
Prepared meat and fish	Group A	174	163	5	n.a.	5	188	6
	Group B	185	161	6	n.a.	18	81	8
Other sugars	Group A	13	10	2	n.a.	1	480	22
	Group B	14	10	2	n.a.	2	220	36
Pasta	Group A	103	92	5	n.a.	6	252	15
	Group B	149	90	5	n.a.	54	149	54
Prepared fruits and vegetables	Group A	131	74	51	n.a.	6	311	15
	Group B	141	72	51	n.a.	18	138	18
Tea and roasted coffee	Group A	27	24	2	n.a.	1	632	19
	Group B	28	23	2	n.a.	3	277	31
Sauces and prepared sauces	Group A	38	35	2	n.a.	1	377	6
	Group B	39	35	2	n.a.	2	157	9
Other food preparations	Group A	40	31	8	n.a.	1	131	4
	Group B	43	31	8	n.a.	4	56	5
Distilled liquor	Group A	114	92	11	n.a.	11	771	77
	Group B	187	89	11	n.a.	87	519	241

continued next page

Appendix Table B.4 (continued)

Product category	Parameter	Consumer surplus gain (A+B+C+D)	Producer surplus loss (A)	Tariff revenue decline (B)	Quota rents eliminated[a] (C)	Efficiency gain (D)	Consumer surplus cost per job[b] (million won)	Efficiency cost per job[c] (million won)
Leaf tobacco	Group A	86	54	9	13	10	925	103
	Group B	116	52	9	13	42	520	187
Natural steatite	Group A	2	1	1	n.a.	0	353	6
	Group B	2	1	1	n.a.	0	146	7
Cosmetics	Group A	29	24	4	n.a.	1	300	15
	Group B	34	24	4	n.a.	6	139	24
Toilet preparations	Group A	2	1	1	n.a.	0	626	13
	Group B	2	1	1	n.a.	0	261	14
Casein	Group A	23	18	4	n.a.	1	289	18
	Group B	27	17	4	n.a.	6	137	28
Plywood	Group A	62	24	36	n.a.	2	379	10
	Group B	64	23	36	n.a.	5	136	11
Wooden tableware and kitchenware	Group A	6	3	3	n.a.	0	72	5
	Group B	8	3	3	n.a.	2	30	7
Carpets	Group A	4	2	2	n.a.	0	184	5
	Group B	5	2	2	n.a.	1	66	6
Apparel	Group A	345	310	23	n.a.	12	70	2
	Group B	411	303	23	n.a.	85	29	6
Other textile articles	Group A	56	49	4	n.a.	3	90	5
	Group B	78	48	4	n.a.	26	43	14
Porcelain household articles	Group A	10	8	1	n.a.	1	50	3
	Group B	13	8	1	n.a.	4	23	7
Glassware	Group A	6	3	3	n.a.	0	139	4
	Group B	7	3	3	n.a.	1	50	4

Glass beads and imitation pearls	Group A	4	1	3	n.a.	0	613	12
	Group B	4	1	3	n.a.	0	216	13
Stoves and ranges	Group A	19	16	2	n.a.	1	237	15
	Group B	24	16	2	n.a.	6	117	28
Steel household articles	Group A	31	28	2	n.a.	1	86	2
	Group B	34	28	2	n.a.	4	38	4
Aluminum household articles	Group A	6	5	1	n.a.	0	102	6
	Group B	8	5	1	n.a.	2	49	10
Motor vehicles for people	Group A	413	393	6	n.a.	14	339	12
	Group B	426	385	6	n.a.	35	143	12
Motor vehicles for goods	Group A	158	137	12	n.a.	9	373	21
	Group B	198	135	-2	n.a.	51	190	49
Electric musical instruments	Group A	6	5	1	n.a.	0	483	28
	Group B	8	4	1	n.a.	3	184	70
Equipment for games	Group A	17	4	13	n.a.	0	619	10
	Group B	18	4	13	n.a.	1	169	11
Sporting goods	Group A	17	9	7	n.a.	1	148	5
	Group B	18	8	7	n.a.	3	49	13

a. Nontariff barriers have not been estimated for some agricultural products nor for any manufactured products. These goods are indicated by "n.a." in the quota rents eliminated column. For purposes of calculating consumer surplus gain, the "n.a." entries are treated as zeros.

b. Consumer cost per job is calculated by dividing consumer surplus gain (A+B+C+D in this table) by the change in employment (preliberalization employment in table B.1 minus post-liberalization employment in table B.3).

c. Efficiency cost per job is calculated by dividing efficiency gain (D in this table) by the change in employment (preliberalization employment in table B.1 minus postliberalization employment in table B.3).

Source: Author's estimates.

References

APEC Secretariat. 1995. *Survey Impediments to Trade and Investment in the APEC Region*. 1995 report by the Pacific Economic Cooperation Council for APEC. Singapore: APEC Secretariat.

Bergsten, C. Fred, Kimberly Ann Elliott, Jeffrey J. Schott, and Wendy E. Takacs. 1987. *Auction Quotas and U.S. Trade Policy*. POLICY ANALYSES IN INTERNATIONAL ECONOMICS 19. Washington: Institute for International Economics.

Burns, Michael E. 1973. "A Note on the Concept and Measure of Consumers' Surplus." *American Economic Review* 63, no.3: 335–44.

Carter, Colin A., and Walter H. Gardiner. 1988. *Elasticities in International Agricultural Trade*. Boulder, CO: Westview Press.

Cho Soon. 1994. *The Dynamics of Korean Economic Development*. Washington: Institute for International Economics.

Choi, Nacgyun. 1993. *The Effects of the UR Agreements on the Korean Industry* (in Korean). Seoul: Korea Institute for Industrial Economics and Trade.

Daewoo Economic Institute. 1994. *The Uruguay Round and the Korean Economy* (in Korean). Seoul: Korea Economic Daily Press.

Deaton, Angus, and John Muellbauer. 1980. *Economics and Consumer Behavior*. Cambridge, UK: Cambridge University Press.

de Melo, Jaime, and David Tarr. 1992. *A General Equilibrium Analysis of U.S. Foreign Trade Policy*. Cambridge, MA: MIT Press.

Economic Planning Board (EPB), Republic of Korea. 1992. *Review of UR Text on Agriculture and Policy Implications* (in Korean). Seoul.

Fukushima, Takashi, and Namdoo Kim. 1989. "Welfare Improving Tariff Changes: A Case of Many Goods and Many Countries." *Journal of International Economics* 26: 383–88.

General Agreement on Tariffs and Trade (GATT). 1992. *Trade Policy Review Mechanism: Korea*. Geneva.

Han, Hong-Yol. 1993. *Characteristics and Effects of the Korea's Market-Opening Policies* (in Korean). Seoul: Korea Institute for International Economic Policy.

Hoekman, Bernard. 1995. *Tentative First Steps: An Assessment of the Uruguay Round Agreement on Services*. Centre for Economic Policy Research Discussion Paper No. 1150. London: CEPR.

Hufbauer, Gary Clyde, and Kimberly Ann Elliott. 1994. *Measuring the Costs of Protection in the United States*. Washington: Institute for International Economics.

Jones, Michael. 1993. "The Geometry of Protectionism in the Imperfect Substitutes Model: A Reminder." *Southern Economic Journal* 60: 235–38.

Kim, Dohoon. 1995. "Price Differentials between Foreign and Domestic Goods and Policy Implications" (in Korean). Paper presented at a conference on Price Stabilization under the System of WTO, sponsored by the Korean Chamber of Commerce, Seoul.

Kim, Kwang-Suk. 1988. *The Economic Effects of Import Liberalization and Industrial Adjustment Policy* (in Korean). Seoul: Korea Development Institute.

Kim, Namdoo. 1994. "Tariffs." In Korea Institute for International Economic Policy, *World Trade Organization and New Trading System: Sectoral Contents and Policy Implications* (in Korean). Seoul: KIEP.

Kim, Namdoo, and Wookhyon Jang. 1996. "Korea's Trading System and Trade Policy." In *The Korean Economy: Current Status and Policy Direction* (in Korean). Seoul: Korea Institute for International Economic Policy.

Korea Customs Service and Korea Customs Research Institute. 1993. *Statistical Yearbook of Foreign Trade 1992*. Seoul: Korea Customs Research Institute.

Korea Foreign Trade Association. 1994. *Guide to Exporting and Importing* (in Korean). Seoul.

Korea Institute for International Economic Policy (KIEP). 1992. *Recent Development and Future Direction of Korea's Trade Policies and System* (in Korean). Seoul.

Korea Institute for International Economic Policy (KIEP). 1994. *The World Trade Organization and the New Trading System: Sectoral Contents and Policy Implications* (in Korean). Seoul.

Korea Rural Economic Institute (KREI). 1991. *Korea's Agricultural Trade Policy after the Uruguay Round* (in Korean). Seoul.

Korea Rural Economic Institute (KREI). 1993. *An Analysis of the Effects of Opening Korea's Agricultural Markets after the Uruguay Round Agreements* (in Korean). Seoul.

Korean Ministry of Agriculture, Forestry, and Fisheries. 1993. *Statistical Yearbook of Agriculture, Forestry, and Fisheries 1992*. Seoul.

Korean Ministry of Agriculture, Forestry, and Fisheries. 1994. *Report on the Uruguay Round and Current Agricultural Policy* (in Korean). Seoul.

Korean Ministry of Finance. 1994. *Recent Development of Korean Industry and Tariff Structure* (in Korean). Seoul.

Korean National Statistical Office. 1991. *Korean Standard Industrial Classification*. Seoul.

Korean National Statistical Office. 1994. *Report on Mining and Manufacturing Survey 1992*. Seoul.

Korean National Statistical Office. 1995. *Major Statistics of the Korean Economy*. Seoul.

Lee, Jae-Ok, Jin-Kyo Seo, and Jung-Bin Lim. 1991. *The Direction of Korea's Trade Policy after the Uruguay Round* (in Korean). Seoul: Korea Rural Economic Institute.

Lee, Won-Young. 1992. *Trade-Industry Model of the Korean Economy* (in Korean). Seoul: Korea Development Institute.

Ministry of International Trade and Industry (MITI), Industry Structure Council, Japan. 1996. *Report on the WTO Consistency of Trade Policies by Major Trading Partners*. Tokyo.

Morkre, Morris, and David Tarr. 1980. *Effects of Restrictions on United States Imports: Five Case Studies and Theory*. Washington: Federal Trade Commission.

Noland, J. Marcus. 1996. *The Future of U.S.-Korea Economic Relations*. APEC Working Paper Series 96-08. Washington: Institute for International Economics.

Pacific Economic Cooperation Council (PECC). 1995. *Survey of Impediments to Trade and Investment in the APEC Region*. Singapore.

Park, Myung-Ho. 1994. *International Comparison of Living Costs and Policy Implications* (in Korean). Seoul: Center for Economic Education, Korea Development Institute.

Rousslang, Donald, and Stephen Parker. 1984. "Cross-Price Elasticities of U.S. Import Demand." *Review of Economics and Statistics* 66: 518–23.

Rousslang, Donald, and J. Suomela. 1985. *Calculating the Consumer and Net Welfare Costs of Import Relief.* USITC Staff Research Study No. 15. Washington: US International Trade Commission.

Sazanami, Yoko, Shujiro Urata, and Hiroki Kawai. 1995. *Measuring the Costs of Protection in Japan.* Washington: Institute for International Economics.

Stern, Robert, Jonathan Francis, and Bruce Schumacher, eds. 1976. *Price Elasticities in International Trade.* London: Trade Policy Research Center.

Tarr, David, and Morris Morkre. 1984. *Aggregate Costs to the United States of Tariffs and Quotas on Imports: General Tariff Cuts and Removal of Quotas on Automobiles, Steel, Sugar, and Textiles.* Washington: Federal Trade Commission.

Yoo, Jung-Ho, Sung-Hoon Hong, and Jae-Ho Lee. 1993. *Korea's Industrial Protection and Distortion of Incentive System* (in Korean). Seoul: Korea Development Institute.

Uruguay Round Schedule LX — Republic of Korea, Agricultural Products. 1994. Part of the Country Schedules annexed to Marrakesh Protocol to the GATT 1994. GATT: Geneva.

US International Trade Commission (USITC). 1989. *The Economic Effects of Significant U.S. Import Restraints, Phase I: Manufacturing.* USITC Publication 2222. Washington.

US International Trade Commission (USITC). 1993. *The Economic Effects of Significant U.S. Import Restraints.* USITC Publication 2699. Washington.

US Trade Representative (USTR). 1996. *National Trade Estimate Report on Foreign Trade Barriers.* Washington.

Yoo, Jung-Ho, Sung-Hoon Hong, and Jae-Ho Lee. 1993. *Korea's Industrial Protection and Distortion of Incentive System* (in Korean). Seoul: Korea Development Institute.

Other Publications from the Institute for International Economics

POLICY ANALYSES IN INTERNATIONAL ECONOMICS Series

1   The Lending Policies of the International Monetary Fund
    John Williamson/*August 1982*
                    ISBN paper 0-88132-000-5   72 pp.

2   "Reciprocity": A New Approach to World Trade Policy?
    William R. Cline/*September 1982*
                    ISBN paper 0-88132-001-3   41 pp.

3   Trade Policy in the 1980s
    C. Fred Bergsten and William R. Cline/*November 1982*
    (out of print)   ISBN paper 0-88132-002-1   84 pp.
    Partially reproduced in the book *Trade Policy in the 1980s.*

4   International Debt and the Stability of the World Economy
    William R. Cline/*September 1983*
                    ISBN paper 0-88132-010-2   134 pp.

5   The Exchange Rate System, Second Edition
    John Williamson/*September 1983, rev. June 1985*
    (out of print)   ISBN paper 0-88132-034-X   61 pp.

6   Economic Sanctions in Support of Foreign Policy Goals
    Gary Clyde Hufbauer and Jeffrey J. Schott/*October 1983*
                    ISBN paper 0-88132-014-5   109 pp.

7   A New SDR Allocation?
    John Williamson/*March 1984* ISBN paper 0-88132-028-5   61 pp.

8   An International Standard for Monetary Stabilization
    Ronald I. McKinnon/*March 1984*
    (out of print)   ISBN paper 0-88132-018-8   108 pp.

9   The Yen/Dollar Agreement: Liberalizing Japanese Capital Markets
    Jeffrey A. Frankel/*December 1984*
                    ISBN paper 0-88132-035-8   86 pp.

10 Bank Lending to Developing Countries: The Policy Alternatives
    C. Fred Bergsten, William R. Cline, and John Williamson/*April 1985*
                    ISBN paper 0-88132-032-3   221 pp.

11 Trading for Growth: The Next Round of Trade Negotiations
    Gary Clyde Hufbauer and Jeffrey J. Schott/*September 1985*
    (out of print)   ISBN paper 0-88132-033-1   109 pp.

12 Financial Intermediation Beyond the Debt Crisis
    Donald R. Lessard and John Williamson/*September 1985*
    (out of print)   ISBN paper 0-88132-021-8   130 pp.

13 The United States-Japan Economic Problem
    C. Fred Bergsten and William R. Cline/*October 1985, 2d ed. January 1987*
    (out of print)   ISBN paper 0-88132-060-9   180 pp.

14 Deficits and the Dollar: The World Economy at Risk
    Stephen Marris/*December 1985, 2d ed. November 1987*
    (out of print)   ISBN paper 0-88132-067-6   415 pp.

15 Trade Policy for Troubled Industries
Gary Clyde Hufbauer and Howard F. Rosen/*March 1986*
ISBN paper 0-88132-020-X   111 pp.

16 The United States and Canada: The Quest for Free Trade
Paul Wonnacott, with an Appendix by John Williamson/*March 1987*
ISBN paper 0-88132-056-0   188 pp.

17 Adjusting to Success: Balance of Payments Policy
in the East Asian NICs
Bela Balassa and John Williamson/*June 1987, rev. April 1990*
ISBN paper 0-88132-101-X   160 pp.

18 Mobilizing Bank Lending to Debtor Countries
William R. Cline/*June 1987*   ISBN paper 0-88132-062-5   100 pp.

19 Auction Quotas and United States Trade Policy
C. Fred Bergsten, Kimberly Ann Elliott, Jeffrey J. Schott,
and Wendy E. Takacs/*September 1987*
ISBN paper 0-88132-050-1   254 pp.

20 Agriculture and the GATT: Rewriting the Rules
Dale E. Hathaway/*September 1987*
ISBN paper 0-88132-052-8   169 pp.

21 Anti-Protection: Changing Forces in United States Trade Politics
I. M. Destler and John S. Odell/*September 1987*
ISBN paper 0-88132-043-9   220 pp.

22 Targets and Indicators: A Blueprint for the International
Coordination of Economic Policy
John Williamson and Marcus H. Miller/*September 1987*
ISBN paper 0-88132-051-X   118 pp.

23 Capital Flight: The Problem and Policy Responses
Donald R. Lessard and John Williamson/*December 1987*
(out of print)   ISBN paper 0-88132-059-5   80 pp.

24 United States-Canada Free Trade: An Evaluation of the Agreement
Jeffrey J. Schott/*April 1988*   ISBN paper 0-88132-072-2   48 pp.

25 Voluntary Approaches to Debt Relief
John Williamson/*September 1988, rev. May 1989*
ISBN paper 0-88132-098-6   80 pp.

26 American Trade Adjustment: The Global Impact
William R. Cline/*March 1989*
ISBN paper 0-88132-095-1   98 pp.

27 More Free Trade Areas?
Jeffrey J. Schott/*May 1989* ISBN paper 0-88132-085-4   88 pp.

28 The Progress of Policy Reform in Latin America
John Williamson/*January 1990*
ISBN paper 0-88132-100-1   106 pp.

29 The Global Trade Negotiations: What Can Be Achieved?
Jeffrey J. Schott/*September 1990*
ISBN paper 0-88132-137-0   72 pp.

30 Economic Policy Coordination: Requiem or Prologue?
Wendy Dobson/*April 1991* ISBN paper 0-88132-102-8   162 pp.

31 The Economic Opening of Eastern Europe
John Williamson/*May 1991* ISBN paper 0-88132-186-9   92 pp.

32 **Eastern Europe and the Soviet Union in the World Economy**
Susan M. Collins and Dani Rodrik/*May 1991*
                    ISBN paper 0-88132-157-5   152 pp.

33 **African Economic Reform: The External Dimension**
Carol Lancaster/*June 1991* ISBN paper 0-88132-096-X   82 pp.

34 **Has the Adjustment Process Worked?**
Paul R. Krugman/*October 1991*
                    ISBN paper 0-88132-116-8   80 pp.

35 **From Soviet disUnion to Eastern Economic Community?**
Oleh Havrylyshyn and John Williamson/*October 1991*
                    ISBN paper 0-88132-192-3   84 pp.

36 **Global Warming: The Economic Stakes**
William R. Cline/*May 1992*   ISBN paper 0-88132-172-9   128 pp.

37 **Trade and Payments After Soviet Disintegration**
John Williamson/*June 1992*   ISBN paper 0-88132-173-7   96 pp.

38 **Trade and Migration: NAFTA and Agriculture**
Philip L. Martin/*October 1993*
                    ISBN paper 0-88132-201-6   160 pp.

39 **The Exchange Rate System and the IMF: A Modest Agenda**
Morris Goldstein/*June 1995*   ISBN paper 0-88132-219-9   104 pp.

40 **What Role for Currency Boards?**
John Williamson/*September 1995*
                    ISBN paper 0-88132-222-9   64 pp.

41 **Predicting External Imbalances for the United States and Japan**
William R. Cline/*September 1995*
                    ISBN paper 0-88132-220-2   104 pp.

42 **Standards and APEC: An Action Agenda**
John S. Wilson/*October 1995*
                    ISBN paper 0-88132-223-7   176 pp.

43 **Fundamental Tax Reform and Border Tax Adjustments**
Gary Clyde Hufbauer assisted by Carol Gabyzon/*January 1996*
                    ISBN paper 0-88132-225-3   108 pp.

44 **Global Telecom Talks: A Trillion Dollar Deal**
Ben A. Petrazzini/*June 1996*   ISBN paper 0-88132-230-X   128 pp.

45 **WTO 2000: Setting the Course for World Trade**
Jeffrey J. Schott/*September 1996*
                    ISBN paper 0-88132-234-2   72 pp.

46 **The National Economic Council: A Work in Progress**
I.M. Destler/*November 1996*
                    ISBN paper 0-88132-239-3   90 pp.

BOOKS

IMF Conditionality
John Williamson, editor/*1983*   ISBN cloth 0-88132-006-4   695 pp.

Trade Policy in the 1980s
William R. Cline, editor/*1983*
(out of print)   ISBN paper 0-88132-031-5   810 pp.

Subsidies in International Trade
Gary Clyde Hufbauer and Joanna Shelton Erb/*1984*
                    ISBN cloth 0-88132-004-8   299 pp.

International Debt: Systemic Risk and Policy Response
William R. Cline/*1984*   ISBN cloth 0-88132-015-3   336 pp.

Trade Protection in the United States: 31 Case Studies
Gary Clyde Hufbauer, Diane E. Berliner, and Kimberly Ann Elliott/*1986*
(out of print)   ISBN paper 0-88132-040-4   371 pp.

Toward Renewed Economic Growth in Latin America
Bela Balassa, Gerardo M. Bueno, Pedro-Pablo Kuczynski,
and Mario Henrique Simonsen/*1986*
(out of stock)   ISBN paper 0-88132-045-5   205 pp.

Capital Flight and Third World Debt
Donald R. Lessard and John Williamson, editors/*1987*
(out of print)   ISBN paper 0-88132-053-6   270 pp.

The Canada-United States Free Trade Agreement:
The Global Impact
Jeffrey J. Schott and Murray G. Smith, editors/*1988*
                               ISBN paper 0-88132-073-0   211 pp.

World Agricultural Trade: Building a Consensus
William M. Miner and Dale E. Hathaway, editors/*1988*
                               ISBN paper 0-88132-071-3   226 pp.

Japan in the World Economy
Bela Balassa and Marcus Noland/*1988*
                               ISBN paper 0-88132-041-2   306 pp.

America in the World Economy: A Strategy for the 1990s
C. Fred Bergsten/*1988*   ISBN cloth 0-88132-089-7   235 pp.
                               ISBN paper 0-88132-082-X   235 pp.

Managing the Dollar: From the Plaza to the Louvre
Yoichi Funabashi/*1988, 2d ed. 1989*
                               ISBN paper 0-88132-097-8   307 pp.

United States External Adjustment and the World Economy
William R. Cline/*May 1989*   ISBN paper 0-88132-048-X   392 pp.

Free Trade Areas and U.S. Trade Policy
Jeffrey J. Schott, editor/*May 1989*   ISBN paper 0-88132-094-3   400 pp.

Dollar Politics: Exchange Rate Policymaking in the United States
I. M. Destler and C. Randall Henning/*September 1989*
(out of print)   ISBN paper 0-88132-079-X   192 pp.

Latin American Adjustment: How Much Has Happened?
John Williamson, editor/*April 1990*
                               ISBN paper 0-88132-125-7   480 pp.

The Future of World Trade in Textiles and Apparel
William R. Cline/*1987, 2d ed. June 1990*
                               ISBN paper 0-88132-110-9   344 pp.

Completing the Uruguay Round: A Results-Oriented Approach
to the GATT Trade Negotiations
Jeffrey J. Schott, editor/*September 1990*
                               ISBN paper 0-88132-130-3   256 pp.

Economic Sanctions Reconsidered (in two volumes)
  Economic Sanctions Reconsidered: Supplemental Case Histories
  Gary Clyde Hufbauer, Jeffrey J. Schott, and Kimberly Ann Elliott/*1985, 2d ed.*
    December 1990   ISBN cloth 0-88132-115-X   928 pp.
                               ISBN paper 0-88132-105-2   928 pp.

  Economic Sanctions Reconsidered: History and Current Policy
  Gary Clyde Hufbauer, Jeffrey J. Schott, and Kimberly Ann Elliott/*December 1990*
                               ISBN cloth 0-88132-136-2   288 pp.
                               ISBN paper 0-88132-140-0   288 pp.

Pacific Basin Developing Countries: Prospects for the Future
Marcus Noland/*January 1991*   ISBN cloth 0-88132-141-9   250 pp.
(out of print)   ISBN paper 0-88132-081-1   250 pp.

Currency Convertibility in Eastern Europe
John Williamson, editor/*October 1991*
                         ISBN paper 0-88132-128-1   396 pp.

International Adjustment and Financing: The Lessons of 1985-1991
C. Fred Bergsten, editor/*January 1992*
                         ISBN paper 0-88132-112-5   336 pp.

North American Free Trade: Issues and Recommendations
Gary Clyde Hufbauer and Jeffrey J. Schott/*April 1992*
                         ISBN paper 0-88132-120-6   392 pp.

Narrowing the U.S. Current Account Deficit
Allen J. Lenz/*June 1992*
(out of print)   ISBN paper 0-88132-103-6   640 pp.

The Economics of Global Warming
William R. Cline/*June 1992*   ISBN paper 0-88132-132-X   416 pp.

U.S. Taxation of International Income: Blueprint for Reform
Gary Clyde Hufbauer, assisted by Joanna M. van Rooij/*October 1992*
                         ISBN cloth 0-88132-178-8   304 pp.
                         ISBN paper 0-88132-134-6   304 pp.

Who's Bashing Whom? Trade Conflict in High-Technology Industries
Laura D'Andrea Tyson/*November 1992*
                         ISBN paper 0-88132-106-0   352 pp.
Korea in the World Economy
Il SaKong/*January 1993*   ISBN paper 0-88132-106-0   328 pp.
Pacific Dynamism and the International Economic System
C. Fred Bergsten and Marcus Noland, editors/*May 1993*
                         ISBN paper 0-88132-196-6   424 pp.

Economic Consequences of Soviet Disintegration
John Williamson, editor/*May 1993*
                         ISBN paper 0-88132-190-7   664 pp.

Reconcilable Differences? United States-Japan Economic Conflict
C. Fred Bergsten and Marcus Noland/*June 1993*
                         ISBN paper 0-88132-129-X   296 pp.

Does Foreign Exchange Intervention Work?
Kathryn M. Dominguez and Jeffrey A. Frankel/*September 1993*
                         ISBN paper 0-88132-104-4   192 pp.

Sizing Up U.S. Export Disincentives
J. David Richardson/*September 1993*
                         ISBN paper 0-88132-107-9   192 pp.

NAFTA: An Assessment
Gary Clyde Hufbauer and Jeffrey J. Schott/*rev. ed. October 1993*
                         ISBN paper 0-88132-199-0   216 pp.

Adjusting to Volatile Energy Prices
Philip K. Verleger, Jr./*November 1993*
                         ISBN paper 0-88132-069-2   288 pp.

The Political Economy of Policy Reform
John Williamson, editor/*January 1994*
                         ISBN paper 0-88132-195-8   624 pp.

Measuring the Costs of Protection in the United States
Gary Clyde Hufbauer and Kimberly Ann Elliott/*January 1994*
ISBN paper 0-88132-108-7   144 pp.

The Dynamics of Korean Economic Development
Cho Soon/*March 1994*   ISBN paper 0-88132-162-1   272 pp.

Reviving the European Union
C. Randall Henning, Eduard Hochreiter and Gary Clyde Hufbauer, editors/*April 1994*
ISBN paper 0-88132-208-3   192 pp.

China in the World Economy
Nicholas R. Lardy/*April 1994*   ISBN paper 0-88132-200-8   176 pp.

Greening the GATT: Trade, Environment, and the Future
Daniel C. Esty/ *July 1994*   ISBN paper 0-88132-205-9   344 pp.

Western Hemisphere Economic Integration
Gary Clyde Hufbauer and Jeffrey J. Schott/*July 1994*
ISBN paper 0-88132-159-1   304 pp.

Currencies and Politics in the United States, Germany, and Japan
C. Randall Henning/*September 1994*
ISBN paper 0-88132-127-3   432 pp.

Estimating Equilibrium Exchange Rates
John Williamson, editor/*September 1994*
ISBN paper 0-88132-076-5   320 pp.

Managing the World Economy: Fifty Years After Bretton Woods
Peter B. Kenen, editor/*September 1994*
ISBN paper 0-88132-212-1   448 pp.

Reciprocity and Retaliation in U.S. Trade Policy
Thomas O. Bayard and Kimberly Ann Elliott/*September 1994*
ISBN paper 0-88132-084-6   528 pp.

The Uruguay Round: An Assessment
Jeffrey J. Schott, assisted by Johanna W. Buurman/*November 1994*
ISBN paper 0-88132-206-7   240 pp.

Measuring the Costs of Protection in Japan
Yoko Sazanami, Shujiro Urata, and Hiroki Kawai/*January 1995*
ISBN paper 0-88132-211-3   96 pp.

Foreign Direct Investment in the United States, Third Edition
Edward M. Graham and Paul R. Krugman/*January 1995*
ISBN paper 0-88132-204-0   232 pp.

The Political Economy of Korea-United States Cooperation
C. Fred Bergsten and Il SaKong, editors/*February 1995*
ISBN paper 0-88132-213-X   128 pp.

International Debt Reexamined
William R. Cline/*February 1995*   ISBN paper 0-88132-083-8   560 pp.
American Trade Politics, Third Edition
I. M. Destler/*April 1995*   ISBN paper 0-88132-215-6   360 pp.

Managing Official Export Credits: The Quest for a Global Regime
John E. Ray/*July 1995*   ISBN paper 0-88132-207-5   344 pp.

Asia Pacific Fusion: Japan's Role in APEC
Yoichi Funabashi/*October 1995*   ISBN paper 0-88132-224-5   312 pp.

Korea-United States Cooperation in the New World Order
C. Fred Bergsten and Il SaKong, editors/*February 1996*
ISBN paper 0-88132-226-1   144 pp.

Why Exports Really Matter!   ISBN paper 0-88132-221-0   34 pp.
Why Exports Matter More!   ISBN paper 0-88132-229-6   36 pp.
J. David Richardson and Karin Rindal/*July 1995; February 1996*

Global Corporations and National Governments
Edward M. Graham/*May 1996*   ISBN paper 0-88132-111-7   168 pp.

Global Economic Leadership and the Group of Seven
C. Fred Bergsten and C. Randall Henning/*May 1996*
ISBN paper 0-88132-218-0   192 pp.

The Trading System After the Uruguay Round
John Whalley and Colleen Hamilton/*July 1996*
ISBN paper 0-88132-131-1   224 pp.

Private Capital Flows to Emerging Markets
After the Mexican Crisis
Guillermo A. Calvo, Morris Goldstein, and Eduard Hochreiter/*September 1996*
ISBN paper 0-88132-232-6   352 pp.

The Crawling Band as an Exchange Rate Regime:
Lessons from Chile, Colombia, and Israel
John Williamson/*September 1996*   ISBN paper 0-88132-231-8   192 pp.

Flying High: Civil Aviation in the Asia Pacific
Gary Clyde Hufbauer and Christopher Findlay/*November 1996*
ISBN paper 0-88132-231-8   232 pp.

Measuring the Costs of Visible Protection in Korea
Namdoo Kim/*November 1996*
ISBN paper 0-88132-236-9   112 pp.

WORKS IN PROGRESS

Liberalizing Financial Services
Michael Aho and Pierre Jacquet

Trade, Jobs, and Income Distribution
William R. Cline

China's Entry to the World Economy
Richard N. Cooper

Corruption and the Global Economy
Kimberly Ann Elliott

Economic Sanctions After the Cold War
Kimberly Ann Elliott, Gary C. Hufbauer and Jeffrey J. Schott

Trade and Labor Standards
Kimberly Ann Elliott and Richard Freeman

Summit of the Americas: A Progress Report
Richard Feinberg

Regional Trading Blocs in the World Economic System
Jeffrey A. Frankel

The New Transatlantic Marketplace:
"Building Blocks," A Free Trade Area, or a North Atlantic APEC?
Ellen Frost

Forecasting Financial Crises: Early Warning Signs for Emerging Markets
Morris Goldstein and Carmen Reinhart

Overseeing Global Capital Markets
Morris Goldstein and Peter Garber

Global Competition Policy
Edward M. Graham and J. David Richardson

The External Face of the European Union
C. Randall Henning

Prospects for Western Hemisphere Free Trade
Gary Clyde Hufbauer and Jeffrey J. Schott

The Future of U.S. Foreign Aid
Carol Lancaster

The Economics of Korean Unification
Marcus Noland

The Case for Trade: A Modern Reconsideration
J. David Richardson

Has International Economic Integration Gone Too Far?
Dani Rodrik

The World Trading System: Challenges Ahead
Jeffrey J. Schott

Canadian customers can order from the Institute or from either:

RENOUF BOOKSTORE	LA LIBERTÉ
1294 Algoma Road	3020 chemin Sainte-Foy
Ottawa, Ontario K1B 3W8	Quebec G1X 3V6
Telephone: 613 741-4333	Telephone: 418 658-3763
Fax: 613 741-5439	Fax: 800 567-5449

Visit our website at: http://www.iie.com

E-mail address: orders@iie.com